Seldom Sung Songs

Seldom Sung Songs

by RAY LOCKE

ROUNDTABLE PUBLISHING, INC.
SANTA MONICA CALIFORNIA

ROUNDTABLE PUBLISHING, INC.
933 Pico Boulevard
Santa Monica, CA 90405

First Printing, 1984

Library of Congress Catalog Card Number — 83-063200

Distributed by:

HIPPOCRENE BOOKS
171 Madison Avenue
New York, NY 10016

PRINTED IN THE UNITED STATES OF AMERICA

To
Donald
Jane
Noel
Kay
And Especially For
Velma Gordon Palmertree

Seldom Sung Songs

1

Three Women at Sunrise

The morning put Lavina in mind of one of those old country songs they played on the radio, one where some white gal was howling about a hurtin' time.

It was a hurting time this morning, the second Monday in May, 1954. It was also Lavina's birthday. Lying awake those few quiet moments she gave herself before getting out of bed every morning, she remembered what day it was, but found no joy in it, no reason to celebrate the passing of another year, not on this day in particular when they were bringing death into Miz Ouida's house. Not, certainly, on the second morning of her own loss. That loss in its enormity crowded lesser hurts, lesser considerations, from her mind as she lay there next to Henry Lambert, her husband of more than a quarter of a century, who, she knew, carried about some sort of alarm clock of his own in his head that would sound off in about twenty minutes and bring him, at once, totally awake and rested.

Out of bed, she dressed quickly, put a pot of coffee on the kitchen stove to boil and broke her fast with cold biscuit and sausage left over from the day before. Then, almost fearfully, she crossed the breezeway that separated one half of the old dogtrot house from the other, and entered Jamie's room. The bed was as she had seen it the last thing before going to her own the night before; as it had been two mornings now, made and covered neat with the white chenille spread. She sat, her weight heavy, on the edge and rubbed her hand, palm down, lightly back and forth across the nubs of the chenille, as if trying to find a lingering warmth left behind by her son. Until two mornings ago, only two mornings, there had lain at rest here a young man . . . No, not quite a young man, but a mature boy bounding quickly into his manhood.

And now the sun peeped over Old Indian Ridge and, as if attracted by Lavina's sorrow, threw a ray stealing in the crack left by the warped window shade, cutting like a knife across Jamie Boy's pillow, and slashed again at the wound that had come visiting to his mother's heart with such suddenness.

It had been only last week, time so short as could be counted in hours, that Jamie got up one morning complaining about the sun waking him up too early.

"Means summer's coming on," Henry had said.

"Means that shade's too narrow for the window and has always been. Next time you go to town, you go in Newberry's and buy a new shade, then," Lavina countered.

Jamie looked at her as if she'd lost her mind. "I don't know beans 'bout buying no window shades. What *size* would I ask for?"

"I'll measure it for you, then you take what I measure to Miss Jewel—that's the woman with that real black hair, wears too much of that old white face powder—and she'll give it to you. You think you can handle a big job like that?"

Now, remembering, Lavina felt warm tears beginning to river her broad African cheeks that were the dark rich color of powdered chocolate. Maryjane started into Jamie's room, hoping to find him there, but stopped as she saw her mother slide to the floor on her knees, fold her hands in silent prayer, and turn a tear-stained face toward the slash of new sun. Lavina was a big woman, big of bone rather than of flesh, and as strong as many men half her age and in their prime. Maryjane had never seen her mother cry before, nor had she ever seen any man cry, but the knowledge slipped into her mind that there would be no difference.

And, a moment later, when Clarise, her ten year old sister, came cackling out of the kitchen, Maryjane quickly crossed the breezeway and pushed her back inside. Innately she knew that Lavina's grief was a deeply private thing and would be shared with no other person, ever.

And in another house that squatted large, Victorian, and ugly atop a gentle rise nine hundred yards to the west, and which was flanked by large pecan trees and flowering plants of more varieties than anyone had ever bothered counting, another grieving woman paused at the kitchen screendoor, as that same new sun found its way to the chinaberry tree in the backyard and turned it into a magical thing appearing to be covered with new golden coins, if only for a moment. Ouida Grace Kantwith hoped it was a good omen. But she really didn't believe in omens. Omens were for fortune tellers and such. And preachers. No, Ouida didn't believe in omens. It had been a long time, now, since she'd been sure in her own mind that she really believed in God.

A hundred and some odd miles to the west and north, still another woman, one who did believe in omens if not in God, woke in a Greenville motel room. She woke smiling, convinced that all her grief was behind her, buried deep in her psyche and deep in the long ago. She greeted the new day with a smile, for today was one that she had looked forward to for more than a decade.

She was, or had been, Kiki Kantwith, a former Ole Miss beauty queen, whose escapades had gained her a lasting notoriety, and many of which had been so original in concept and execution that among certain people she was still spoken about with something akin to reverence. Then, a dozen or so years before, when World War II was at its zenith, she had simply disappeared.

One rumor had it that she had been captured by the Japanese, charged with espionage, and tortured to death in a most revolting manner. Another had it that an Arabian prince had kidnapped her to his harem, where she had grown fat and ugly and the mother of a new child yearly. The rumors had so amused both Kiki and her late husband that on more than one occasion they had added one of their own to the litany.

None of this wild speculation ever came close to the truth. She had merely taken, as a first husband, a young soldier, an extremely handsome and boring boy from Kansas, and followed him from one godawful army air base to the next, finding herself in Santa Fe, New Mexico, and with a job exercising horses on a dude ranch, when he was sent overseas to pilot a fighter plane. He was killed only a few days before Germany fell, which was just as well, as she had already chosen her second husband. Canton Boles Chislom was well on his way to becoming one of the richest men in the world when he fell in love and married for the first time at nearly fifty years of age. Kiki went home with him to Houston, where she quickly became one of River Oaks' more popular hostesses, a staunch supporter of the arts and a world traveler, friend of senators, governors, and, yes, an Arab prince or two.

There had always been a few vague rumors about Katherine Chislom, something about a former marriage and some sort of college age transgressions of propriety. However, Houston society had never dug too deeply into such things; primarily in fear of finding a mirror that was somewhat more tarnished.

Of course there were people scattered here and there in the South—and elsewhere—who knew that Kiki Kantwith and Katherine Chislom were one and the same. And if it mattered a twit, they went along with the joke.

Among those who were not in on the joke, had never given much more than a passing moment's thought as to what happened to his baby sister, but who knew and revered the Chislom name as much as his own, was Thomas Kantwith. And just about the time she stepped into the shower in the Greenville motel, Tom sat down to breakfast a hundred and some odd miles to the east and south.

Had he bothered to look out the kitchen window, he would have seen Lavina Lambert leave her house by the front door and start up the rise to what she always referred to as Miz Ouida's house. This worry about a missing son and the bringing home of Miz Ouida's dead son to be buried opened other wounds of grief long safely tucked away in the corners of her mind. That week, the year before Jamie was born, when her three oldest children had died, one by one, of diphtheria, came rushing back to her consciousness with a suddenness and vividness that almost staggered her. For no good reason she could think of, she began softly singing:

Good news . . .
Chariot's coming . . .
Good news . . .

2

Dead Two Years

Ouida was waiting for Lavina near the chinaberry tree, watching her walking, long of stride and deliberate of step, on past the barn and toward the house. Lavina, as always, wore a loose-fitting cotton house dress that buttoned down the front and an old straw hat, fading red in color, with black dragons stenciled on its wide brim, and tied beneath her chin with a braided cord. The women were friends, had been for many years, and closer than either of them would ever admit, even to each other. They had long since lost the need to exchange a lot of words.

"Morning, Lavina. You hear anything about Jamie?"

Lavina's eyes searched the other's face for a long moment. At forty-five plus a month, a year and some younger then herself, Ouida Kantwith was still a pretty woman, going to a pleasant roundness rather than fat. Today her eyes were circled dark and carried a darting fear and dread in them.

"No'm. Did you? Did he say anything about it?"

"He said he hadn't heard anything." Ouida looked away and then continued: "Said boys Jamie's age are always running off after some woman."

"Not my Jamie. He's a good boy."

"I know, and I'm sure there's some *reason* . . . He's going to come back. I'm sure that's true." But Ouida wasn't sure of any such thing, and they both knew it. "Can I borrow your hat for the garden? I can't find my old hat anyplace. Did you see it?"

Lavina stifled a chuckle. Ouida Kantwith was forever misplacing things, most often her straw hat. She untied the cord of the faded red hat and took it off. As Ouida reached for it, she grimaced in pain and quickly grabbed her right arm near the shoulder.

"What's the matter with you?"

"I don't know . . . This old arm of mine. I woke up in the middle of the night with a pain in it just awful. I never had that pain there before . . ."

"Nerves. That's what it is," Lavina said. "Best you put it out of your mind. You going to town to meet the train they bringing him on?"

"No. No," Ouida answered, taking the hat and putting it on her head. It was much too large. "I saw him leave home from the front porch the last time. I guess I'll see him come home the last time from the same place."

Lavina nodded and started on toward the house. Ouida picked up her garden baskets and the shears and then paused, looking at the sky. "It's going to get a lot hotter today," she said to no one in particular. Lavina turned for a moment and resisted the urge to run after the woman and hold her and tell her it would be all right. But how did you go about telling a woman that burying a son was going to be anything except what it was? For all she knew, her own son was lying dead someplace, as dead as Perce Kantwith. And he'd been dead two years already.

"Lavina?"

"Ma'm?"

"You know who I woke up thinking about this morning?"

The answer seemed obvious to Lavina, but rather than say the name of Ouida's dead son, she politely asked: "Who?"

"Kiki. Prissy, pretty little Kiki Kantwith. Isn't that odd?"

Lavina again kept what she thought of as the obvious answer to herself. "Ain't a day goes by I don't think of Miss Kiki," she said softly and continued on toward the house.

Tom Kantwith, a handsome man nearing fifty but still carrying the weight and measurements of his youth, had finished his breakfast and was sitting at the kitchen table staring out the window, when Lavina entered the room through the back porch door. From the table at the front of the kitchen he could see the garden and, beyond, the combination service station and grocery store that he owned where the road curved at the bottom of the hill and continued on up to Old Indian Ridge, past Hebron Methodist Church and his Aunt Iola's house, then absorbing other roads, passing two decaying hamlets and eventually joining the Natchez Trace down in the southeast corner of the Bogue Chitto country.

Lavina cleared the breakfast dishes from the table and poured a fresh cup of coffee for Tom. They didn't speak, not this morning or any other, if words could be avoided. As worried as she was about Jamie, and as much as she knew that hardly anything went on in Bogue Chitto without Tom Kantwith knowing about or being a part of it, she did not for a moment entertain the idea of asking him, nor the notion that he would answer her if she did. The truth was, they hated each other with a hatred that was as pure as a baby's love and as clear as one of Miz Ouida's crystal glasses. Lavina had always suspected that Tom Kantwith only insisted that his wife do all the cooking, because he was convinced that she would poison him if she got the chance. It had become something of a joke between the women, for unbeknownst to Tom, Lavina actually did more of the cooking in the Kantwith house than Miz Ouida did.

"That goddam Billy Ray Waters. I ought to shoot him."

Lavina grunted. She'd heard that threat before, at least a hundred times.

"Middle of the morning and he still ain't opened my store for business." Lavina grunted again. She couldn't see why it was all that important that Billy Ray Waters open the store at sunrise, as no one traded there but people who worked for Tom or lived on his land and needed credit from him. That was most of the people who lived in the Bogue Chitto country, but for the most part they did their trading late in the day, when the work was done, or on Saturday. In fact Tom Kantwith vehemently insisted they do their trading, even in his store, on their own time.

"I'm going over yonder and get his ass out of bed one last time—what's that woman standing down there staring at?"

Lavina walked over and looked out the window. "Who? Miz Ouida?"

"Now who else you know would be standing down there in our garden staring at the pole beans?"

"Staring at her thoughts, I suspect," Lavina said and returned to the breakfast dishes. Tom looked at her as if she'd gone crazy, got up from the table, and left the house.

Indeed, Ouida was staring at the pole beans: Two years. Two years dead. The words kept running through her mind. Perce had been dead two years, and it's like having him die all over again . . .

Perce would have liked to come home on a day like this one, with the sun shining hot and the birds singing in the bushes about the house the way they were doing early this morning. He would have liked that, having a choice in the matter . . . not that any of us have a choice in when we die. Or when we're brought home to rest either. Not these days. There's no power on earth that can stop us from dying when the time comes, not even the United States government. *Especially* the United States government.

I can't ever stop thinking about Perce for the life of me, it seems. And now that they're bringing him home, I think about how that boy could feel about a day like this and let you know how he felt, even make you feel the same way just a little bit . . . He had that power. He knew of it—creation. And he wanted to know more. All about it. About Heaven and the stars; about elements and the earth. He was forever wondering about such things and asking questions that nobody I knew had the answer to, not even his teachers. Just thinking about him can get me thinking about such things all the quicker than any preacher could ever do. About how God made Heaven, and He made the earth and the trees and the hills. Light and dark and the sheep and the little fish, and then he went a step farther and He made us in His image, it's said. (However, I have never believed He—Him being all what they say He is—could do all that in seven days.)

They say we're supposed to be best of the lot. You take all the killing and hurting that man does, one to the other, does that sound like something the best made would do? No. It appears to me sometimes like we may be the worst of the lot. Such as lying and cheating and hurting and killing can't be laid at the feet of the sheep, which He made. And the wars . . .

That's the worst of it, the wars. I can't for the life of me see why a bunch of grown men would want to take up arms one against the other. Terrible arms. Worse than that, I can't see how a bunch of elected congressmen and what all has got the right to tell men they have to take up those terrible arms . . .

Now you take my Perce, my baby, whose body they are bringing back here today from where it has lain these two years on a mountainside across the seas in Korea. He never wanted to take up arms against no Chinamen or Koreans. He hadn't ever seen a Korean that I know of and I've not either. I don't have the want of seeing one of them either. But Perce, he *knew* about them. There wasn't much he didn't know something about . . .

But one of them that probably had no more want of killing people than Perce did . . . One shot and killed him, my Perce. More than likely the Lord made the heathen Chinamen for a purpose just like they say He made us. But I don't see how come He made us all take up arms one against the other, and kill I don't know how many of one another . . . Kill my Perce who never hurt a living thing in his life . . . Kill my beautiful baby. Shot dead over there on some battlefield where he didn't want to be. Where he had no business being, not Perce.

Lord.

Even as a baby Perce had been special, not just my first born, but a very special little creature. I could bring him down here in this very garden and put him over there in the shade, and he'd just laugh and coo and carry on like he was having the best time in the world. That was the year I—

That had been the year Ouida left Tom; had taken Perce and gone back up to Lodi, in northern Montgomery County, and stayed for nearly six months with her parents in the comfortable old house where she'd been born and grown up as the only child of loving, if somewhat stern, Presbyterian parents, who had insisted that she go as far in school as possible, probably because they thought she was too plain and timid to ever find a husband. After she'd finished Lodi School, they'd sent her to Kilmichael to live with her father's sister Edna and get her high school diploma, and then on to Blue Mountain for two years' teacher's training.

She'd been hired straight out of Blue Mountain to come to this Bogue Chitto land to teach first and second grades at Green Grove School by Tom's Aunt Iola, who was the principal and crazy as a loon, even back then. That was in the fall of 1929, and Iola had arranged for her to board here at Kantwith, with Tom's parents and pretty little Kiki, just a child starting school herself.

Flattered out of good sense that the tall, handsome Kantwith son would pay one iota of attention to the mousey thing she felt herself to be, much less pay court to her, she hadn't hesitated a moment when he proposed. They'd been married in the wisteria arbor when the school term was out, with Kiki serving as the prettiest little flower girl any bride ever had.

Perce had been conceived right away, and it was while she was carrying him that she found out about Tom's women—Carroll County honkytonk women, and even others who found the Kantwith looks, charm, and money hard to resist. And when Perce had been born—as handsome as any Kantwith that ever lived—she'd grown tired of Tom's staying away from home almost all of every weekend, embarrassed by the solicitous sympathy of her mother-in-law, the half-hearted excuses his father made for Tom's long absences. So she'd packed Perce up and taken him home to Lodi. Only to shock her parents and make them feel uncomfortable.

For the next six months Tom had spent his weekends courting her again, begging her to come back to Kantwith. Finally she'd given in; it was the last independent thing Ouida Grace Kantwith had done in her life, up until the time Perce was killed. After that, pleasing Tom hadn't seemed as important anymore.

Lord. Perce was a good boy—and smart. In that way his sister Camilla takes after him. He read poetry and could write it too. Yes, and he was the first person I ever knew in my whole life who could do that.

Lord.

Things just weren't the same here after Perce went off to war. It was just as if the goodness had been cut out of us with a knife, without him being here to help out, to make it all seem prettier than it was, somehow . . . Then came the day of my life I will never forget, the day old Jasper Morgan brought me that telegram. It was the first and last telegram I ever got in my life, and I pray to the Lord—if there is a Lord—that I never get another one.

All it said was that my beautiful baby was dead. My Perce was dead over there, so far away from home, and me not hardly being able to believe that my son, my Perce, could of died such a young death without me knowing about it the minute it happened.

They sent me money.

Just like it would make up for him. Ten thousand dollars made out to me like Perce told them to do. Dollar hungry as Tom Kantwith is, he's never said one word about that ten thousand dollars.

Maybe it will be easier now, with them bringing him home. Having him buried over there in Hebron Church graveyard that I can see on the hill from my own front porch, having him there with all his kin, will make me feel a lot better about it. Knowing at least his resting place is not halfway around the world from me . . . That will give me some peace of mind—

"Who are you talking to out here by yourself?" Tom was standing at the garden gate.

"Was I talking to somebody?"

"You been standing there talking to that row of pole beans for the last half hour at least."

"Maybe I'm talking to myself. And to the trees and this old garden, and maybe to the Lord," Ouida answered.

"Some people would say you were crazy, if they heard you talking to yourself."

"Some people would be a lot better off saying some of the things they got to say to themselves, instead of blabbering them to everybody they know . . . You not gone yet? You better get started if you're going to talk to Old Man Goodwin before that train comes in—"

"It's that damned Billy Ray Waters. I am going to run that damned Waters family off my land, is what I'm about to do."

"What did Billy Ray do now?"

"It's what he's not doing's the problem. Half the morning's gone, and he was still laying around in bed when I went over there and got him up."

"You worry less about Billy Ray Waters and more about your own son. You want to be late meeting his train? There ought to be one member of this family there to meet the train."

"I don't reckon he'll be likely to run off no place if I ain't there on the dot to meet the train."

Ouida resisted the temptation to swear at him. She began picking the stringbeans and said quietly: "That is about the meanest thing I ever heard you say."

"Billy Ray Waters would stand up to you and dispute that this morning." He laughed: "He sure would do that."

"You just be there to meet that train, Tom."

"I'll be there, I told you. All I have to do is stop in the Bolatusha Bank and talk to Old Man Goodwin a few minutes. I'm buying that old Crenshaw place."

"Now what on earth do you want with that worn out old farm? I swear it would seem like you are trying to buy up every acre of land in Mississippi."

"It's going to be worth money someday."

"I'd like to know what for? It's not a thing but a bunch of gullies and scrub pine trees. Half the land you own now ain't worth paying the taxes on, it would seem to me like."

"Mark my word, land around here is going to be worth plenty one of these days. And I happen to know it won't be too far off, that day."

"More likely you're going to make us so land poor we'll end up living off the County . . . You better get going. I've got a million things to do. I've got to go over to the church and make sure they dig the grave in the right place, otherwise they'll put him Lord knows where—"

"What time did Bud say he and Hazel would get here?"

"Not likely before late morning or maybe even dinner time. They said they were stopping to spend the night with Hazel's folks up there in Memphis. They weren't leaving Chicago until yesterday morning."

"It will be good to see them . . . ole Bud."

"It would be good to see Perce too . . . You be there to meet that train."

"I'm going. I'm going," he said and began walking away.

"Tom?"

"What?"

"See if you can find out anything about what happened to Lavina's boy. Will you?"

"I ain't studying Lavina's boy."

3

Stranger in the Wisteria Arbor

Lavina was standing, with arms folded, watching Ouida and Tom in the garden, when Camilla came into the kitchen and slammed the door.

"Lord God Almighty, Camilla! You liked to scared me to death! What are you doing home from school anyway?"

"I got the day off because of Perce."

"Ain't you got them tests?"

"Next week is test week."

"Don't watch out you won't be graduating with your class. They leave you behind."

"More than likely I'm going to be the valedictorian. I don't think I have to worry too much about getting left behind." She, a thin, not unpretty girl of sixteen, walked over and turned on the kitchen radio.

"Now Camilla, don't you be turning that thing up so high. I don't feel like listening to all that old loud nigger music you play this morning."

"That ain't no nigger. That's Johnnie Ray. He's white."

"He the one all the time howlin' about some cloud crying?"

"Yep."

"I don't care *what* he is, I can't stand him the worst. Now turn that thing down before I shut it off for you."

"You fixing that breakfast for me?"

"Well I ain't fixing it for no ghost."

"Just one egg then. I don't feel hungry."

"Was that Progress Whittal's car I seen up here last night?"

"Progress Whittal. Ain't that a name for the record books? You know what the kids in school used to call him? *Prog*. Old Prog. They could call him Gress I reckon. I got my own name for him. Sure not *Progress*."

"What are you talking out of your head this morning, girl? Ain't he up here sparking you most every night lately?"

"Is that what they call it? I just wish the damned slob would keep his ticket at home—"

"You watch that cussing, girl. I done warned you about that talking nasty."

"If you had to sit out on the porch swing half the night and listen to that frog croak, with pimples all over his face that you can see them in the dark, you'd cuss too, I bet."

"I'd just tell the young man go home, if I felt that way bout him."

"Lavina, you know who the young man in question is, and you know who his father is, surely you know that?"

"He's that boy of Mr. Joiner Whittal. Ain't nobody in Bogue Chitto *don't* know that. Old man Whittal is so rich he don't know how much money he *has* got, is what they say."

"I know what he's got. He's got one ugly child named Progress, more land than Tom Kantwith's got, and he's got cancer. He's also got a man who sat here and ate breakfast not long ago paying a whole lot of attention to him of late and especially to his frog-faced son."

"What you saying, girl?" Lavina asked, as she dumped the scrambled egg on a plate. The portents here were getting a little dark, a little foreboding, for her taste.

"What I'm saying is that Daddy Tom owns about half of Bogue Chitto, and Mr. Joiner owns most of the other half, and he's got cancer—"

"Uh oh. I don't like none of this—"

"Un huh. And Daddy Tom figures, if he can fix me up with the only living Joiner heir, why hell, he's gonna get his greedy hands on the whole shebang. Not that anybody is going to bother writing it up in the Jackson *Daily News* if he does. Not once they got a good look at the Bogue Chitto anyway."

"Child, someday your daddy is gonna walk in on you sassing him like that, and he's gonna slap you down. I think you just making all this stuff up in your head in the first place."

"Sure I am."

"Maybe your daddy just wants to see you well fixed."

"If Tom Kantwith would turn loose a dollar now and then, I'd be as well fixed as anybody this side of Memphis, without any of this business he's got in mind with old Prog Whittal. You know what he's gone and done now?"

"Who, Progress Whittal?" Lavina asked. She was watching Ouida coming up from the garden, laden with two baskets of fresh vegetables.

"Hell no. Tom."

"Honey, I ain't studying what your daddy's up to. Here comes your mama, you better stop that sassy talk."

"He put Prog up to asking me to let him take me to the fund raising carnival at school tonight. Now can't you just see me showing up at a dance at the school with old Progress Whittal? Far as I know he's never had a real date with a girl in his life."

"Far as I know the same can be said about you and boys," Lavina said, and immediately wished she could bite the words back when she saw the tears spring into Camilla's eyes. "Camilla, honey, I didn't *mean*—"

"I *know* what you meant," she said and slammed out the side door that led to the wisteria arbor, just as Ouida arrived at the back porch carrying her baskets. Lavina opened the door for her.

"Was that Camilla?" Ouida asked. "I almost forgot that she was staying home today."

"That was her all right. And I had to go and open my big mouth. Miz Ouida, you better have a talk with that girl."

"A talk? What do you mean, a talk?"

"I mean a talking to. A woman to woman talk—"

"You mean about . . . ?"

"That too, what with pimply-faced lil' old Whittal boys hanging around here on your front porch wearing out they welcome. What I'm telling you is, that child has had a lot frozen up inside herself for too long!"

"She's just upset because of Perce. We *all* are . . ."

"That's just what I'm telling you. She's just grieving over Perce enough that . . . that . . ." Lavina couldn't find the words. "That she's *crying*!"

"Well that seems like the perfectly natural thing to do to me—"

"Like every other woman standing under the roof of this house, that girl is about two shakes from a breakdown. That is a growing woman out there, Miz Ouida, and she *needs* you!"

"Well can't you talk to her?"

"No'm I can't. I'm about talked out. You her mother, and it's a mother she's needing now."

"Oh. I'll see what I can say to her," Ouida answered and walked out the door that led to the arbor. Lavina picked up the baskets of vegetables and carried them to the sink. "Sometimes I could just shake that woman," she muttered to herself.

"Camilla?" Ouida said, taking a seat beside her daughter on the white painted wooden bench beneath the wisteria. "Are you crying?"

"No . . . yes."

"What's wrong?" Ouida asked, as she folded her hands in her own lap and stared down at them. She had always found it difficult to touch, to hold her children, once they'd passed the age of asking to be held.

"Nothing. Lavina just reminded me that I've never been on a real date with a boy."

"Well of course you have. You've been to football games and things."

"With a bunch of kids. A real date, mama, is when a boy comes and picks up a girl in a car and takes her to a picture show in Winona or skating, or to a dance or something."

"Oh well. You have plenty of time for that. You're still a little—"

"Don't tell me I'm still a little girl again, mama. I will be seventeen years old, come December first. Two girls I went to grade school at Green Grove with have got babies already."

"Well, you wouldn't want to have a baby, surely?" She looked up through the bright and lacy green leaves over her head at the pale blue sky. It really was a nice day for Perce to come home.

"I think you probably have to have a date before you have a baby. At least I think that's the way it's done."

"Well, I really don't see why . . . what . . . is so upsetting about it. Anyway I didn't think— I wouldn't think you'd be so worried about something like that on this day," Ouida said.

"Well, the first time I'm ever asked for a date—a real date—in my whole life is by a boy who is about twenty years old who is too dumb to come in out of the rain and has never yet that I know of found a girl who'd be seen dead at a dog fight with him, that's all."

"Did Progress ask you to go someplace with him? Your father will be pleased."

"*That* is exactly the point, mama! Tom Kantwith put that asshole up—"

"Camilla!"

"—up to asking me to go to the May Carnival with him at the high school gym tonight," Camilla spat through clenched teeth. "Can't you just see that? The senior class's candidate for May Queen showing up with the All American creep? I'd get laughed right out of that gym. And you know who put him up to asking me? Tom Kantwith, that is who."

"Well, you're not going. With your brother lying in yonder in his coffin he'll be and you off to a carnival."

"I didn't *say* anything about going. I just said that the only time I've ever been asked for a date in my life was by somebody nobody in the state of Mississippi would be seen dead with, and Tom Kantwith put him up to it. That's what I'm saying. Mama, did he go to meet the train they're bringing Perce on?"

"He went," Ouida answered. "And you go put on a decent dress and take off them shorts."

"It's too hot for a dress."

"People will be coming out here to pay respects when the body gets here . . . What are they going to say if they catch you dressed like that?"

"People have got so much to say about this family in particular already, they are not going to pay any attention to how I'm dressed. They are going to be watching Daddy Tom to see what words of wisdom come out of the vile, vulgar mouth of his, is what people are going to be doing."

"Be quiet. Someday that big mouth of yours is going to get you in more trouble than it can talk its way out of."

"Besides," Camilla said, tears welling up in her eyes again, "it's not as if it was a real funeral. A real funeral . . . A real funeral is for somebody just after they have died. Perce has been dead for over two years, and all we are doing is moving him from one place to the other."

Ouida's voice was soft, barely more than a whisper, when she turned to her daughter and spoke next: "Be quiet now, Camilla. I told you to be quiet. It doesn't matter how long your brother has been dead, his funeral means just as much as it would have meant if we could of had it when he died. I doubt if they put much stock in a proper Christian burying in times of battle. And if you had any respect for the memory of your brother, you wouldn't be acting so sassy . . . And go put on a dress. Shorts don't strike my mind as decent public wear no time, and much less today. What will the people say?"

"Nothing. They'll be too busy watching to see if Tom Kantwith auctions the flowers right off Perce's grave to pay any attention to me," Camilla answered.

"Show some respect for your father."

"Why should I? What have I got to respect him for? For fixing me up with ole Progress Whittal? You can't tell me he'd be hanging around here unless Tom Kantwith put him up to it. Too bad this is not a hundred years ago and he could just haul off and give me to ole Prog outright . . . or maybe swap me even for some of ole Joiner's land."

Camilla, angry and hurt, looked away from her mother: "Or maybe I should respect him for going off and getting drunk as a dog every Saturday night and raising hell with old Mavis Patton in that jukejoint of hers over there on Vaiden road, huh? Like he has been doing once a week for the past twenty years, the way I hear it. You think he will invite that old whore to Perce's funeral?"

"Camilla, please . . . Please stop now. You shouldn't be talking about these things," Ouida pleaded softly.

"I know. I'm not even supposed to *know* about these things. But I do, mama. I know a lot, and I'll say any damn thing I want to about Tom Kantwith, because there is nobody around here got enough respect for him to tell him what I say."

"Someday he is going to hear you talking like that, young lady, and he'll slap your face for you. You know he'd do it."

"When that day comes, he's going to have to have a long reach, because one day soon I am going to go so far away from here nobody will know I'm Tom Kantwith's daughter. They won't even have ever heard of him. That is what's going to happen one day in the near future."

"Now don't start that again, Camilla," Ouida pleaded.

"May as well. The days I can bear to stay under the same roof with him and put up with what he has now begun to refer to as the courtship and future match of great importance to this part of Mississippi are numbered. As if anybody would give a damn. People in town wouldn't stop to think about it, even if I was fool enough to marry Progress Whittal, which will never happen as long as I'm in my right mind. It wouldn't make one blessed difference to nobody but a bunch of Bogue Chitto hicks who work for Tom or ole Joiner Whittal."

"You don't have to talk about that now, Camilla!"

"I *do* have to talk about it, mama! I have to talk!"

"Not now when all I can think about is them bringing your brother home. Don't talk about all that to me, and your leaving too."

"Perce left! Perce left, and Tom grieves him coming home. He wasn't drafted into the army. He joined to get out from under the roof of this house!" She shouted loud enough for Lavina to hear her in the kitchen. "And yesterday—

"Yesterday over at Bolatusha he was going around telling everybody how sad he was, how *heartbroken* he was that they were bringing his oldest son home in a box—"

"Camilla, allow him his grief!"

"Perce hated him, and you know it, and if he could have heard Tom going around carrying on the way he was doing yesterday, he'd jump right out of his coffin! He hated him so much he couldn't contain his hate, and you know that is true, mama."

Ouida stood up, tears blinding her eyes, and staggered toward the kitchen, only to find Lavina, hands on hips, blocking her way.

"Ouida Grace Kantwith! You set yourself right back down there and listen to that child!"

"Well, she's not making any sense, Lavina!"

"Well, she's not making any sense, Lavina," the black woman mocked, in perfect imitation of a cultured East Mississippi white lady. "If you'd open your *ears*, she'd make sense to you. That child's eaten up with old misery she's been holding in herself a long time, and it's gonna come out—"

"But there's so much to be done. They're bringing Perce home."

"Everybody *knows* they're bringing Perce home. And there ain't a thing that has got to be done that I can't do myself. Perce is *dead*, woman! He don't need you no more. If I have to, I'll latch you out of the house," she said, as she turned on a heel and stalked back toward the arbor door.

"Camilla . . . ?"

Staring vacantly at the pink-blooming hydrangea at the edge of the lawn, Camilla said quietly, "You know it's true, mama. Perce hated him. As much as I do, if that's possible—"

"Camilla . . . it's not true."

"It is and you know it. You know how I know? Because Perce was the one that taught it to me. One winter night, oh, far back as I can remember, Tom came home drunk. It was a Saturday, because it had been very cold, and Perce and Bud were home from school, and Tom came home late and drunk. Coming home from Old Mavis Patton even then, but we didn't know about that . . . *You* knew about it, mama. You knew and pretended what everybody else knew wasn't true. Just like you do now . . ."

She pushed a loose strand of dark blonde hair from her face and turned to stare directly at her mother: "I remember that night. He yelled at us and sent us to bed, and when Perce wouldn't go, he slapped him. Then he hit you, mama. More than once. Lots of times. Remember, mama? I'll bet he still smelled of that whore when he beat you . . . I was scared and got into Perce's bed and we lay there listening to you cry . . . The earliest thing I remember in my life, mama, was listening to you cry—

"Maybe Bud listened too. I don't remember. And Perce was crying. Not because he had been slapped by that bastard, but because he was hitting *you*!"

"Camilla, stop it! I don't have to—I won't listen to this!"

Camilla stood quickly and grabbed her mother by the arms. "I don't care if you listen anymore! You never ever listened to me, to any of us, anyway. And if you do listen, you don't *hear*! But

Perce was crying because *Tom Kantwith was our father*! And he said, 'I hate him! *I hate him!*'"

Ouida backed away from Camilla and sank back down on the bench. At the arbor door Lavina felt the ache of Camilla's release and turned to go upstairs and make the beds.

"He told me to say it. Do you know what Perce told me, mama? He said when he got big enough to get some money of his own he would pay me—give me a dime for every time I said I hated Tom Kantwith. He did!

"But he told me he would hit me if I ever said it where Tom could hear me . . . and I never did. Boy, if Perce had ever paid off, I would be rich right now, I can tell you—"

Ouida was staring at her daughter, tears running down her cheeks, her fingers spreading across her mouth, as if she was really seeing her for the first time. For, in a way, she had just encountered a stranger in the wisteria arbor. "Be quiet, Camilla, please . . . Hush, now . . ."

But there was no stopping, not now. "And even before I was sent to school for the first day to be taught anything, Perce had taught me the lesson I had to learn for all time. To hate Tom Kantwith so hard it made me hurt inside, hating him. And I loved Perce. I loved him so much . . ."

She sank to her knees and reached for Ouida's hands. "Mama I loved him. And I can't bear for them to bring that box here today."

Ouida reached and embraced her daughter for the first time in years and slowly began rocking back and forth.

"Mama! I loved him, God I loved him. You don't know how I loved him, mama. And I loved him more because we shared everything, even our hate of Tom. Bud, he was left out of it. Did you know that? We shared things, me and Perce . . . Bud was a son of a bitching tattletale even then—"

"Camilla."

Pulling back to arms' distance, Camilla went on: "You want to hear something, mama? You want to know a game we made up, me and Perce? We used to look at magazines and catalogs . . . We used to find pictures of men. Sometimes we would even cut them out of those books and carry them around in our pockets. At least

I did. Do you know why, mama? You want to know why we carried paperdolls around in our pockets? We would pretend they were our fathers, instead of Tom. Perce thought it up, and we used to hide those paperdoll fathers—ours—we would hide them and take them out at night, and sometimes when Perce didn't have to work, we would talk about our paperdoll fathers and how they . . . they were doctors or something, and we lived in cities and places . . . Places Perce would read about in books and tell me about. And how good they were to you, our paperdoll fathers! How proud we were of them, introducing them to our teachers and people!"

"Please, Camilla—"

"And then sometimes we'd get out the mail order catalogs . . . We played this game. Each of us would get one wish on each page, and we pretended our fathers would buy us the things we wanted on that page. Mama, you . . . if you could only have seen all the clothes and things we wished for you! The stuff we picked out for you would have filled ten houses!

"One time when I was little, Lavina caught me doing it, wishing out of one of those books, and she asked me what I was doing, and I told her. I told her all about it, and she never told anyone. Not even you."

"Be quiet about it now, Camilla. It was just a child's game. All children play such games."

"It was . . . And I stopped playing it when I was in the sixth grade. Perce had stopped playing it long before, I guess. Remember how he started keeping to himself so much in those times?

"I stopped playing it the day Daddy Tom came to school to get me when grandma died. You remember that, mama? When Grannie Kantwith died? Tom walked right into that old schoolroom, where old Mrs. Mitchell taught, just like he was God Almighty in the flesh, him looking mean, and said: 'I've come to get my girl, Camilla. Her Grannie is dead.' That is exactly what he said. Then he looked old Mrs. Mitchell up and down and asked her how much of a kickback she was getting out of all those workbooks she was making us buy, and a lot of other nasty foul things to her. Mama, he made that old woman cry. Him with enough money to buy the factory that put out those workbooks, making that old woman cry because of thirty-five cents . . . And scaring all those other little kids half to death. That was when I stopped playing games, mama. You can't pretend anymore after everyone you go to school with has seen your shame. Mama, I am still going to school with that same class, and old Mrs. Mitchell is still teaching and telling every one of her classes about the time Tom Kantwith came into her room—telling them that he is an evil man, and how he sweats the blood of his own kind and turns it into money, which he uses to scare people. Just to scare and bully them . . .

"But they know better in town, don't think they don't. They know of him because of what he has, but they also know him for what he is. Mama, I really think the only reason the senior class elected me their candidate for May Queen was just to see if Tom would turn loose enough money for me to win . . . or even to buy me a decent dress to wear to the thing—"

"Camilla, I have money. I can buy you a dress, if it's that important. Why didn't you tell me?"

"That's not the point, mama."

"He can't help it. He can't help being what he is, Camilla. It's shameful to talk like this now. With your brother's body coming home today."

"No. No, it is not. It is not shameful, mama. It's not disrespectful to Perce. I just hope he is where he can see what meets his body at that train this day—how really miserable and selfish and mean he's become."

Ouida thought a moment before she spoke again, choosing her words carefully and deliberately: "Tom can't help what he is," she said. "An obsession like his, about buying up all this old worthless land, all these old worn out farms, and never spending any money on anything else—maybe, once something like that gets into a man's blood he can't control it anymore. The oddest thing is, I don't know how it ever got started with Tom.

"But he loves you, Camilla. I do believe that."

"Sure. Like he loved Aunt Kiki? I guess he loved her so much he drove her off from home, and she's never come back—"

"That was different. Something different."

"Is that why he's pushing me on creepy old Progress Whittal? Because he *loves* me?" Camilla asked.

"Tom wants what he thinks is best for you. I won't make

excuses for him, because he's always thought he's known what was best for others. And you being his only daughter . . ."

"He doesn't know what is best for me. And I think he has some notions of getting more out of pushing old Progress off on me than what he thinks of as my happiness."

"He loves you, Camilla. He loved Perce too, in his way, but his love is different from that of most people. I think Perce loved him too. I really do think that."

Camilla looked at her mother. "Maybe he pitied him, mama, but that is not love."

"Perce had a lot of pity in his heart, and he had a lot of love that maybe you never did see, Camilla. Maybe you weren't old enough to see the love that was there, but it was there. I have to believe that."

Camilla saw that she really did have to believe that.

"Now go wash your face. And put a dress on. Please?"

"Yes'm."

"Did you hear something?"

"Sounded like a car pulling up out front."

The blood drained from Ouida's face. "It couldn't be—"

"No, mama. The train doesn't get into Winona for nearly two hours."

"That's right, isn't it? I better go see who it is. But I'm not ready for company, not yet . . ."

4

What Young Old Man Goodwin Told

The banker, Old Man Goodwin, was not really an old man at all. He was, at thirty-six, more than a decade younger than Tom Kantwith. But his father, who had also been the banker at Bolatusha and who had also been called Old Man Goodwin, died, leaving both the bank and the appellation to young Donald.

He pulled up into the drive, cut the ignition off, and stared at the house sitting before him. The house sat at the level of a gentle slope, a spur of Old Indian Ridge, and faced west, overlooking the store and Bogue Chitto Bottom. There had always been a certain oddness about the place, not quite sinister but certainly unwelcoming. It was, actually, an ugly house, looking vaguely New England and out of place. Kiki Kantwith had once described it as "two large boxes, one stood on its side, the other on its end and then which someone tried to make look for all the world like a wedding cake."

She had not been far off. Shadowland, as the place had been known as in his grandfather's day and was still so referred to in all the pertaining legal documents, did look like an ungainly wedding cake with all its Victorian bric-a-brac hanging from every corner and cornice that would support it.

No one, not even the old timers, called the place Shadowland anymore. That had long since been replaced by "the Kantwith place," or "Kantwith's Store," and, finally, just "Kantwith."

Although he had not been out here in years, it amazed Donald Goodwin how little the place ever changed. Of course there had been one change when he came back from the war; Kiki Kantwith was no longer here. Gone never to return. At least not until today. He, like many Bogue Chitto men of his generation, had once been in love with Kiki. He still found much about her that he liked, even admired. He opened the car door and got out.

At the same time, the woman once known as Kiki Kantwith was having her second cup of very strong coffee in the sun filtered patio of a beautifully groomed and walled plantation house garden located just outside Greenwood. Her hostess, and old friend and onetime college roommate, was saying: "I still think it was downright perverse of you to spend the night in a *motel* room. Why, if nothing else, I could have had someone go over and drive your car on in for you, if you were *that* tired. Besides, there is not a motel in all of the Delta fit for a woman to stay in."

The woman who had been Kiki smiled and sipped her coffee. And her hostess was struck, once again, with the sheer magnificence of this creature. She had always been beautiful, stunningly so, even in their college days. But then there had been a rowdiness about her, a central Mississippi rough edge that hadn't yet been rounded off.

And, of course, there had been that perfectly bizarre family background; an old and respected name that went back to Indian days—and beyond, for they were supposedly descended from a Choctaw princess or something of the sort—on her mother's side, and an English carpetbagger—the first Mississippi Kantwith—with a particularly odious reputation in the father's background. It was said that Kiki's brother—an extraordinarily good looking son-of-a-bitch, if she recalled—had quite capably carried on the Kantwith male tradition of chicanery.

Now, however, there was about Katherine Chislom an elegance that was eloquent in its understatement. Long of limb and thin of body, she wore a simple silk shirtwaist blouse and a khaki-colored skirt that accented her tan, as did the lightly streaked dark blonde hair that was parted on the right and worn straight to the shoulders. Her only jewelry was a very small, very expensive watch, and a pale lip color and barely perceivable eye makeup completed a look that had become a part of Katherine Chislom's persona. It was as if she had totally reinvented herself.

"A goddamn thoroughbred," the woman's husband, a Kentucky-bred gentleman, had once described Katherine, who looked at her watch, set her coffee cup down, and said: "I'd better be on my way."

"Now Katherine. You will come back for a visit after this dreadful funeral business won't you?"

The woman who had been Kiki laughed. "I very well may be back *before* this dreadful funeral business. The last time I saw my brother we didn't exactly take our leave on the best of terms." She stood up to go. "Although, I must say, I don't entirely look forward to this trip to Shadowland with total apprehension."

The other woman shivered visibly. "Is something wrong?" Katherine asked.

"No . . . ," she smiled. "I guess someone just stepped on my gravesite." But, of course, that wasn't it at all. There had been something so utterly cold, so completely soulless in Katherine's last statement, that it had sent a chill up her spine.

As she walked away, waving goodbye, the woman wondered what it would be like to cross Katherine Kantwith Chislom. She quickly put the thought out of her mind. That was something one didn't even think about.

Not unless one was Donald Goodwin. He knew. And that was exactly what he was thinking about, as he stood in the wide sloping yard of the Kantwith house, seven miles southeast of Bolatusha, and wondered what madness had compelled him to come here in the first place.

Behind the lace curtain of the front door window, Ouida was waiting for him to come up the steps before she opened the door. The last time she had seen Donald Goodwin standing on the front lawn of Shadowland holding something in his hand, if she recalled correctly, he had been bringing Kiki home from a date of some sort. It was the year before Kiki left.

That had been a very long time ago, and she could not recall what Donald had been holding in his hand. Nor, in the sun's glare, could she see what it was he held in his hand now. However, there was something disturbing about seeing him standing there on this morning, at this moment. And for a long time, as she stared through the Irish lace at him, she couldn't remember what it was. Then she remembered. Of course. Of course. Tom had left early to meet the train that was bringing Perce because he'd intended to stop in Bolatusha and talk some business with Old Man Goodwin at the bank. In that case, what was Old Man Goodwin doing standing in the front yard?

"Mr. Goodwin?" Ouida said, opening the door.

"Good morning, Miss Ouida. A very nice morning . . . Of course I'm deeply grieved about Perce. What a fine boy he was. I always said that boy would make something of himself one day. He was a lot like you—"

"Mr. Goodwin, what are you doing *here*? I . . . Pardon me, but I really didn't mean for that to come out like it did. It's just a surprise to see you *here*, when I'm quite sure my husband told me he'd gone to town to see you *there*."

"Is that a fact? It must have slipped my mind that he was going to see me there. Otherwise, why would I be here? May I come in for a moment, Miss Ouida?"

"Of course . . . Do come in," she answered, holding he door wide, as he bounded up the steps and across the porch. "Pay no attention to my manners. I'm not myself this morning."

"And little wonder. This must be a terrible burden on you."

"It is," Ouida answered, as she absently opened the doors to the seldom used formal parlor, with its heavy Italian furniture, the silk Persian rug, and the pump organ. She quicky closed the door and backed away. That was where they would be putting Perce, and she really wasn't ready to sit in that room. Not yet. "Let's go into the living room, Mr. Goodwin. It will be much more comfortable." And it was.

"Is something the matter, Mr. Goodwin? Why do I have the feeling that you're here with bad news? It isn't about my money, is it? You know, with this craziness my husband has about buying up land, I'm always worried—"

"Miss Ouida, no one can touch your money—a bit over sixteen thousand dollars, isn't it? Except for yourself and Camilla when she reaches twenty-one—or before, in the unlikely event of your death. No, that is not why I'm here."

"I'm sure my husband told me he was going to meet you at the bank. He said something about buying that old Crenshaw place. Now why old earth would Ira and Doris Crenshaw want to sell out?"

"Because Mr. Kantwith offered them about three times what the place is worth."

"Goodness. Why?"

"And yes, I confess, I was supposed to meet him at the bank. But by being here I can avoid telling him that we can't lend him any more money to buy land—"

"Well, thank goodness for that. I was just telling him this morning that he has more land now than he ever has time to set foot on. It's like he's gone land crazy."

"In a way he has . . . Do you mind if I smoke?"

"Please. But can you tell me why Tom has gone here and there and everywhere buying up every worthless old farm in Bogue Chitto it seems like, for . . . how many years has it been, Mr. Goodwin?"

"About nine or so is my guess."

"Yes, nine. Can you tell me why?"

"Oh, God. I wish I had stayed at the bank and told your husband I couldn't lend him the money to buy any more farms—or at least made some excuse. My late father very freely loaned Mr. Kantwith a great deal of money. He has title to farms over in Choctaw County, even a couple up in Montgomery and over in Carroll. One or two in Attala."

"We must be very much in debt. Mr. Goodwin?"

"Yes."

"Even this place is mortgaged?"

"Yes."

"I'm not the least bit surprised. What I am surprised about is that you'd pick this day to come out here and tell me this," Ouida said.

"That is not what I came out here to tell you. Not at all—"

"But as long as you've told me this much, maybe you should tell me how the bank could afford to loan my husband so much money to buy land?"

"My late father. Until he passed on two years ago, he let Mr. Kantwith have a free hand, you might say. Miss Ouida, do you understand anything at all about banking?"

"Not a thing, I'm afraid. You put money in the bank, and you take it out. And when you've taken out all you put in, then there isn't anymore."

"Well, yes. And you borrow money on property you own to buy more property, and perhaps you even borrow money on *that* property to buy even more—"

"I understand. And that is what my husband has been doing. But you still haven't explained—answered my question. How could the bank afford to loan so much money on land, which, apparently, my husband has been paying too much for?"

"I didn't say too much for all of it. Just in the case of the Crenshaw place and a few other more recent transactions. And who can say what that land will be worth ten years from now: However . . . Miss Ouida, have you ever heard the term factoring? No? Well, in banking sometimes it is possible and even desirable to factor certain transactions, perhaps loans or property, to a third party—a party, say, that would look upon those loans as a good investment—"

"I see. But I don't understand. And you have been factoring my husband's loans to a party that looks upon them as a good investment—is that what you're telling me?"

"Miss Ouida, as a banker there are certain trusts I can't betray. As a matter of fact, I am betraying one by coming out here this morning to tell you . . . what I have to tell you."

"And just what on earth is that, Mr. Goodwin?"

"Miss Ouida, I have always held you in the utmost esteem. You know, I remember the first time I ever saw you? The year you came down from Montgomery County to teach first grade at Green Grove. I was just a kid then, seems like—"

"The next year Perce was born . . . ," Ouida said, glancing out the window toward Old Indian Ridge and remembering that she still had to go over to Hebron and make sure they were digging the grave where she wanted it. "Mr. Goodwin, I trust you didn't come out here . . . What did you come out here to tell me?"

"I guess I am standing here talking around it. You see, I've always respected and admired you, and I know you must have gone through a great deal of pain and suffering these . . . this last couple of years. So . . ." He took a deep breath. "So I've taken it upon myself to prepare you for what may come to you as a shock and come at a very bad time. The very worst time, in fact." The last words were rushed out.

"Mr. Goodwin, you're not making a bit more sense than most

of the conversation I just had with my daughter, Camilla. What shock could be worse than having a son die twice? That's what it's like, Mr. Goodwin, them bringing his body home after all this time. Like having him die all over again."

"Miss Ouida. Kiki is coming home."

The woman stared at him, uncomprehending.

"Kiki? Home?"

"Your sister-in-law. Miss Kiki. She is coming home."

"Home? You mean *here*?" The possible ramifications, the consequences of such an event, rushed through Ouida's mind with the force, wildness, and speed of the Big Black River in spring flood. "When?" she asked.

"Today."

"Today . . . *Today*! Mr. Goodwin, you can't mean today!"

"Miss Ouida, get hold of yourself."

"Mama? Is something the matter?" Camilla asked, coming in from the hallway. "Oh, good morning, Mr. Goodwin. What is it, mama?"

"All these years, I always expected she would come back one day. But of all the days in a lifetime to pick, she had to go and pick this day."

"Who, mama? Who's coming back?"

"Your Aunt Kiki. Mr. Goodwin has brought the news that your Aunt Kiki is coming here today."

"Today?"

"Mr. Goodwin. How did you come by this information?"

"I am betraying a trust by telling you that she is coming. But I thought it was the Christian thing to do, to warn you. Under the circumstances." And to hell with the consequences, he thought—and wondered what Miss Ouida would say if she knew that he'd been entertained in Katherine Chislom's home not three months ago?

"Then my husband doesn't know she's coming?"

"I don't see how that would be possible. As far as I know, everyone that expects her is in this room."

"She is so beautiful in the pictures we have of her," Camilla said.

"Yes. She was a pretty girl . . . I don't know how I'm going to tell Tom she's coming," Ouida replied.

"I had rather you didn't, Miss Ouida. I wanted to warn you about it, but it sure would be a big favor to me if you'd just forget that I told you, where Mr. Kantwith is concerned. Of course that is up to you."

"Yes . . . Let me think about it. When will she be getting here, you think?"

"I don't have the slightest idea," Old Man Goodwin replied.

"He's not going to like it very much, is he? I mean, her coming here?" Camilla asked, and Donald Goodwin could have sworn she was suppressing a smile.

"I don't know what he will say about it. I really don't. All these years since she's left, and never once has he mentioned her name. Not one time."

"Mama, what happened? I mean, between her and Daddy Tom? Why did she leave?"

"It doesn't concern you, Camilla."

"Well, if she's going to be here, I ought to at least know why she left, don't you think? I've heard she was pregnant."

Donald Goodwin turned and looked out the window. Though he'd been in California, in the Army Tank corps, he knew most of what happened the night Kiki left home. What he didn't know was some of the grim details his father could never bring himself to tell. He supposed only Kiki knew those now.

"Your aunt and your father had a falling out, and she left home. They've never seen or spoken to each other since," Ouida said.

"I wonder why she's coming now?" Camilla asked. Donald had been wondering the same thing for several days, and while he suspected he knew the answer, he couldn't bring himself to believe that Kiki could be that cruel.

"After all these years. I wonder too," Ouida said. "The Lord only knows why Kiki Kantwith ever did anything, but she sure picked herself a fine day for coming, what with them bringing Perce home, and that soldier that's coming with the body I already offered to put up, and your brother Bud and Hazel coming any minute now. I don't know where on earth I'm going to sleep her."

"Miss Ouida, my wife and I would be glad to have Kiki stay with us," Donald Goodwin heard himself saying.

"Thank you, Mr. Goodwin. Perhaps . . . It's just like her not to give a person a minute's notice she's coming."

Donald—Old Man Goodwin—saw that Ouida would be able to cope. Tom, without a doubt, would not, and he wasn't sure that he would be capable of coping with Katherine Chislom. But Ouida would. He quickly took his leave.

Ouida followed him to the front steps. "I think it would be best if I didn't mention your visit to my husband," she said. "But I do thank you for coming."

About two miles away, in front of the long abandoned Green Grove schoolhouse, Goodwin met a car carrying Illinois license plates. It was headed toward Kantwith at a very high speed. Driving it was Binford Kantwith, the one they always called Bud, born two years after Perce and, even as a child, as unlike his brother as two members of the same family could possibly be.

5

The Only Living Son

Twenty-two years old his last birthday, Bud Kantwith had not, as they were fond to put it in that part of Mississippi, "found himself." There were those, even in his own family, who doubted he ever would.

Never much of a student, when he graduated from high school at almost nineteen years of age, he went to Memphis and found a job in a warehouse. Although he often talked of going on to college someday, he knew that he never would, and both his parents thought it just as well he didn't, although for entirely different reasons: Ouida was quite sure he'd never cut the grade; Tom was quite sure he didn't want to help pay for the attempt.

A year after he moved to Memphis, Bud met Hazel Bates, a cashier at the Toddle House restaurant on Madison Avenue, and married her five months later. It was another six months before they got up the nerve to take Hazel's aunt up on her invitation to move to Chicago. They'd hoped to find better jobs—which they had—but living with Hazel's aunt hadn't worked out too well, and they now lived in an apartment house where babies cried during the night and people swore at each other early in the morning.

Those were the bare facts of Bud and Hazel Kantwith's existence. However, as they left the miles behind them, driving south, they became blurred, an abstraction, and the closer they got to Bolatusha, Mississippi, the less gritty those facts became. Each mile brought to the mind another veneer of glamor, another notch of success, so that by the time they actually reached

Bolatusha, they were each convinced they'd left a virtual Eden behind, to subject themselves to a backwater experience too dismal to be endured.

However, when they stopped at Harvey's Standard Station and Cafe on the outskirts of Bolatusha, owned by the father of a boy Bud had gone to high school with, he, at least, quickly made a return to reality.

This was when Bevo Harvey took him aside and, while Hazel was using the cafe restroom, told him as much as he could about some of the more interesting things Tom Kantwith had been up to lately. Among the rumors Bevo passed on were those concerning some monstrous amount of land, certain secret dealings with oil companies, and the forthcoming marriage of his sister Camilla to Progress Whittal, which was expected to be announced at any moment. Bud promised Bevo that he would return to Bolatusha to hear more, just as soon as he could dump a pregnant and whining wife off at Kantwith.

It was, of course, their car that left Donald Goodwin eating dust for a full half-mile past Green Grove School and came speeding down the gravel road toward Kantwith's store, as Camilla was walking out on the front porch with a basket of lima beams, which she intended to shell while sitting in the swing on the sunny side of the porch.

"Mama. It looks like Bud's car. I don't know anyone else fool enough to drive that fast on a gravel road."

Ouida came out of the house. "Well, if it is him, he ought to slow down. At that rate they can still see his dust in Bolatusha."

"They're going to beat them here with Perce."

Ouida looked at her daughter: "That's a strange thing to say. What difference does it make?"

"None I guess. I just had it in my mind's eye that when they came driving up here with Perce's—you know—it would be before anybody else got here. For some reason."

Smoothing her hair and tugging at her apron, Ouida walked to the steps. "It will be good to see Bud . . . It's been six months since they were here last fall. And you try and see if you can't get along with Hazel, for once."

"I thought Bud said then they were going to get a new car just as soon as they got back to Chicago," Camilla said, as the Illinois car pulled into the graveled driveway and came to an abrupt halt. "I see Hazel is frowning already."

Ouida didn't hear her, for she was already rushing down the steps to greet the couple getting out of the car: "Why Bud and Hazel! I was just wondering when you all were ever going to get here—"

"Hello, mama," Bud said, hugging her, as he waved his greeting to Camilla, who—as originally intended—had taken her seat in the porch swing and started shelling the lima beans. For no reason she could—or would—think of she felt lonely. No, not lonely, but alone—detached from the noisy greeting ritual that was taking place below her in the yard. She also felt that if she said too much, if she had to talk to anyone about this day, about Perce and what was happening, she would start crying again.

"Hazel! Just look at you!" Ouida said, too loudly. She still wasn't sure how she felt about grandchildren.

"We drove straight through from Hazel's folks," Bud said.

"Here, let me help you with those bags . . . Hazel, don't you go picking up that bag in your condition. Camilla, you come out here and get that bag."

"I got them, mama," Bud said. Camilla remained seated in the swing, pretending she was less interested than she was and, at the same time, somewhat amazed at the dress Hazel wore, a bright red affair with a voluminous skirt and a little bolero jacket with white dots all over it. She was seven months pregnant, and the dress and white shoes with the very high heels were decidedly not maternity wear.

"I'm so glad you all are here," Ouida said, leading the way up the steps. "It was good that you could take your vacation now."

"We had already planned to take our vacation now. We was going to Florida," Hazel said, smirking in Camilla's direction.

"Oh?"

"It's all right, mama. A couple of days won't make that much difference."

"You planning on going on from here?" Ouida asked.

"We already got reservations in a hotel in Tampa," Hazel replied, again throwing a smirk in Camilla's direction. "You too stuck up to speak to someone, is that it?"

"Hello Hazel. Hello Bud."

"When will they be getting here with it . . . him?" Bud asked quickly.

"Not for a while yet—sometime after twelve. He's going to be on the eleven-fifty train. Your daddy went over there to meet him . . . Did you all eat yet?"

"We stopped and got something not long ago," Bud replied. "Hazel got a craving for a hamburger. You know how these new mamas are. . ."

"Well, I'll have Lavina make us some fresh ice tea," Ouida said as she entered the house, followed by Bud. Hazel lingered on the porch, taking a handkerchief out of her purse and wiping her face. "It is so hot here I don't believe it. I'll bet it is a hundred and ten in that old house."

"It ain't nothing yet. Wait until it comes July."

"I won't be here then, thank God for small favors. We got air conditioning in Chicago." With that she flounced through the front door and into the wide hallway.

And not two minutes later Bud came out of the same door, quietly closing the screen behind himself. "Well, little sister, how you doing?"

Camilla looked at him, wary as a fox with pups. She had never particularly liked her brother and had certainly never trusted him—not this brother, who was two years younger and so much different from Perce. "What can I say? Nobody has asked me to be in the next Montgomery Clift picture show."

"Well," said Bud, taking a seat in one of the white painted porch chairs. "From what I hear, you are really getting to be something."

"Is that a fact?"

"I mean being May Queen and all. Mama wrote you was a candidate. Did you win?"

"She *wrote* . . . The contest is tonight."

"Oh. I'll bet you win."

"I wouldn't go betting my last dollar on it if I was you—"

"I hear you got yourself a boyfriend. That's what I hear."

"If you're talking about Progress Whittal, I wouldn't exactly call him a boyfriend, either."

"Uh huh. Way I hear it, him and you are getting to be pretty thick. Way I hear it, Daddy Tom is just about ready to make the announcement."

"Huh?" Camilla said, dropping the lima bean she was shelling. "Now don't you go making any bets on that one either. Or buying no wedding presents, until you find yourself a more reliable source of information."

"Well, you could do worse than ole Prog."

Camilla stared at him for a moment before replying. She couldn't exactly figure out his game, as he had never shown any interest in her or her affairs in the past, that she could recall. "You know, Bud, that may be true. Maybe—just maybe—I could do worse than ole Prog, but right off hand I really can't think of *what* would be worse," she said, as she watched Bud take out a Lucky Strike, light it, and pull the smoke in deeply. "Besides, when the time comes—if it comes—I hope to do a helluva lot better. Now give me one of your cigarettes."

Bud handed her the pack of Luckies. She took two, one for her mouth and one for her shirt pocket.

"Keep'em. I got more in the car."

"They got lots more down at the store, but two is about my limit. How come you twisting around all the time acting so nervous?"

"Look," he said, standing up. "I got some business over at Bolatusha to attend to? I got to see Bevo. I'm going over to the cafe and wait there until they come by with the . . . with Perce. You think they'll come through Bolatusha or by the Vaiden road?"

"How would I know? What are you up to, Bud?"

"Look," he said, now in a hurry. "If Hazel wants to know where I am, tell her. Okay?"

"Boy, you just go around asking for trouble, don't you?" Camilla asked, as he walked quickly toward the car.

"What?"

"You know damn well she's going to be mad as hell when she finds out you're gone. How come I have to do your dirty work for you?"

"I just don't want her tagging around after me, that's all."

"Well, why don't you just come right out and tell her?" Camilla asked teasingly, knowing full well why.

"That's a lot easier said than done."

"I'll bet it is. You're henpecked, you know that, Bud. Just plain ole henpecked."

"I ain't. I just don't want her tagging along everywhere I go."

"I think I might be able to understand that—"

"Look, I got to get going. You tell her, okay?"

"What choice have I got? Where is she anyway?"

"I dunno. Talking to mama or changing her clothes, or something—"

"Bud, didn't it ever occur to you that you might ought to stay here and talk to mama or something?"

His hand was on the handle of the car door. He turned and looked at Camilla. "Well, uh . . . I mean, she's got you and Hazel to talk to. How come there is any need of me being around to talk to her?"

"Well, you know, being as you're the only living son and all that I thought maybe you might think of something to say to her . . . other than hello-goodbye, you know?"

"Well, hell, Camilla. There'll be plenty of time to talk about it later on, won't they?"

"I suppose," she answered, as he got into the car, quickly turned it around, and speeded off back in the direction of Bolatusha. He was hardly past the store when Hazel came running onto the porch, calling his name. She had changed into a yellow chiffon cocktail dress.

"Where . . . ?" She turned to Camilla, her face a fury. "Where is he going?"

Camilla considered the question a moment. "What exactly do you mean?" she asked, watching the car barreling down the gravel road away from Shadowland.

"Are you dumb or what? Where is he going, is what I want to know."

"Dumb? I'm not the one that married Bud Kantwith, am I?"

"Now just what do you mean by that?"

"What I mean by that is there are not a whole lot of people in this world who'd have to stay around Bud for more than an hour to figure out that he's about as stupid as he is selfish."

"That's a pretty awful thing to say about your only living

brother. I got a good mind to tell Miss Ouida on you."

"Tell all you want. I don't give a cat's butt what you tell."

"Well, are you gonna tell me where he's gone to or not?"

"Oh, where has ole Bud gone? Or is it where is he going, since I doubt if he's there yet, even as fast as that fool drives—"

"*Where*, I asked you!"

"I guess you did," Camilla said, looking up at her for the first time since she returned to the porch. The sight of the yellow cocktail dress, with the beading around the neckline, took her aback for a moment.

"You gone deaf or what?" Hazel asked, deliberately flouncing the skirt of the dress.

"No. Just surprised to see all that yellow chiffon on this front porch—and hung on a pregnant woman at that."

"You make me so mad I could just come over there and slap you!"

"You ever lay a hand on me, you're gonna draw back a nub, and don't you forget it, sister. Your silly ass dumb husband said he was going to Bolatusha."

"What for, I'd like to know?"

"For to see Bevo Harvey he told me."

"*Who* is Bevo Harvey?"

"You sure ask a lot of questions for a woman with a smartass mouth. Bevo Harvey is the son of Lennie Harvey, who owns Harvey's Standard Station and Cafe, which is located just this side of Bolatusha at the forks of the highway and the road you took to come out here. Now does that answer your question?"

"We just *came* from there. We stopped there already. How come he'd want to go back there?" Hazel was beginning to turn red behind her freckles.

"To see Bevo Harvey, I told you. How you and Bud got together is becoming less of a mystery to me all the time."

"Well what would he want to see this Bevo Harvey about?"

"Good God. How do you expect me to know. Bevo is an ole boy Bud went to school with, and they used to run around together all the time. Before he went off to Memphis and you all got married."

"Well. You make it sound like we done something wrong."

"Did you?"

"You think you are so smart. What did Bud go to see this boy about? Is he a big ole ugly boy with a red face?"

"That sounds about right. That sounds about right for about half the male population of Bogue Chitto, however."

"Well he just talked to him on our way in here! How come he would want to go back over there and talk to him again?"

"Now how would I know? For all I know maybe he wants to talk about old times. You know, when they were boys and used to jack off together in the barn loft."

"Jesus Christ! You have got a disgusting mouth on you!"

"Look, why don't you either go back in the house and pester mama, or else sit down and shut up and let me shell these lima beans for Lavina? I have never in my whole life studied keeping up with your husband, and I see no good reason to start in now."

"Oh!" Hazel hissed. "It is just like him. To run off and leave me here, a hundred miles from nowhere."

"I guess he does it all the time, huh?"

"What?"

"Runs off and leaves you?"

"No," Hazel lied. "You just wait until he gets back."

"Guess I'll have to."

"I wanted to go for a ride. It's hotter in that old house than it is out here on this porch, I swear. I don't see how on earth you can sit there in that hot sun like you're doing."

"I'm trying to get some suntan."

"A tan isn't becoming to my complexion, my beautician says. Some people get so dark you don't hardly know what race they belong to." She spread the full chiffon skirt over the front steps, as she sat down in the shade.

"I see you changed your dress," Camilla said. The truth was, she was just a bit envious of that dress.

"I don't see what business it is of yours if a person changes her frock."

"Well pardon me all the hell for living."

"Why ain't you in school today?"

"I got off . . ." She suddenly shouted: "A lizard! A big ole green lizard just run up under you!"

Hazel screamed and jumped up, giving Camilla a fright for a moment, as it looked as if she was going to fall off the top of the steps, teetering in her high heels.

"Get it! Get it!"

"Where! Where is it? Get it off! I just can't stand the crawly old things. Where did it go?"

"Oh, you probably scared that thing halfway to Jackson, the way you carry on. I wouldn't worry about it."

"There ain't no lizard, is there? You just said that to scare me!"

"I did?" Camilla asked, smirking and taking up the lima beans again. "You ought to seen yourself jump when you thought a lizard was headed for your fanny."

"You are a mean little tramp, do you know that? I'm going to call your mama!" And she did, bellowing: "Miss Ouida! Miss Ouida!"

"Miss Ouida . . . Miss Ouida. Jesus Christ. You are going to wake up half of Hebron cemetery."

"*Miss Ouida*! Camilla scared me, telling me a nasty old lizard had run up my dress. You hear me, Miss Ouida!"

"Good God."

Ouida opened the screen door, stuck her head out far enough to see Camilla, and asked: "What on earth is the matter with you, Camilla Jean Kantwith? Causing all that commotion at a time like this? And put that cigarette down!"

"I forgot."

"Telling poor Hazel that an ole lizard run up her skirt," she continued, opening the door wider. "What *is* the matter with you today? She's tired after such a long trip, and her condition . . . You want poor Hazel and Bud's baby to be born looking like a lizard?"

Camilla didn't find that image all that displeasing and answered too quickly: "Suit its disposition, if it takes after its parents."

"Did you hear that!" Hazel squealed.

This time Ouida came out onto the porch. "Now Camilla, I've heard just about all I intend to out of that big mouth of yours this morning. Talking that way is showing disrespect for Bud and Hazel, as well as for my poor Perce who'll be coming up that road out there for the last time in a little while. Now you tell Hazel you are sorry, young lady. You hear me?"

"I'm sorry," Camilla said.

"And say it like you mean it, too. I just don't know what has gotten into you this morning. And get those beans done, and put on some decent clothes before they all get here, you hear me?"

"Yes'm."

"Well take those lima beans in the kitchen, and go do what I say. Don't just sit there."

"In a minute."

"I better not have to come back out here and tell you again. You're acting like . . . like some I don't know what this morning." She looked off across the wide plain that was called Bogue Chitto Bottom, called so after the meandering creek that snaked back and forth—often nearly back upon itself—for countless miles through open bottomland and swamps before it finally joined the Big Black River down near Pickens. Cloud shadows now danced across the bottomland, shade splashing the fields of young corn and cotton. In the spring the creek, larger than some called rivers, would often flood to a width of a mile or more, spreading what looked like, from the porch of the house on its high land, a carpet the color of new honey.

On the other side of the Bottom, the road ran almost straight, past the old Green Grove School and on to Bolatusha. Beyond that it joined other roads that led north and west to Montgomery and Carroll counties and to Winona, where the Illinois Central and the Columbus & Greenville railroads junctioned. That was where they would be bringing Perce, where Tom would meet him along with Boswell Thomson and his son Dennis, from the Bolatusha Funeral Home.

Ouida could never look up that way, to the northwest, and not be reminded of more gentle times, more gentle places, of a small L-shaped house that stood across the road from the Lodi School, of blue and white dresses so permeated with flour starch that they could, literally, stand by themselves, of Saturday visits to Winona and holiday visits to relatives in the gracious old town of Carrollton.

Even now, after twenty-five years, she still didn't always feel entirely at home in this Kantwith house, in this dark and sudden Bogue Chitto country, a land isolated and mostly forgotten and turned in on itself and nearly, still, and wild as it had been more than a century before, when soulless outlaws with names like

Harpe, Merrill, and Mason preyed the Old Natchez Trace that was its eastern boundry. Lying between the headwaters of the Big Black and Pearl rivers, it had always been such, a wild and often lawless land. In the late 1700s, the French and English traders—Cravat, Leflore, Palmertree, Allen, Pitchlynn, Folsom, Locke, and Cole, to name a few—came up the Trace to do commerce with the Choctaw and Chickasaw Indians and soon found that the quickest and easiest way to gain favor was to marry the daughter of an important headman or chief. Later came the English and Scot settlers from the Natchez District, farmers for the most part—Gibson, Hunt, Peeler, Gordon, Curtis, Yaeger, Kent, Greenlee, Montague. Later, after the Choctaw Removal of the 1830s, came the Scotch-Irish Presbyterians and English Episcopalians from Virginia and the Carolinas—Cannon, Thomas, Braswell, Grice, Ellis, Austin, Jenkins, McElroy, Burden, Black, White, Wood, and Woods, and dozens of others to mingle with earlier bloodlines.

Still others, like Isaac Kantwith, the first of that name to arrive in Mississippi, came after the Civil War, with enough money in pocket to acquire title to farms and lands from a people too impoverished by the War to pay taxes. Some of these—Isaac Kantwith and his younger brother, Barton—stayed and married into the old families, as would their sons and gradsons.

Tom Kantwith was Isaac's grandson, and Bud, now, would be the last of that branch of the family to carry on the name. Besides Barton's descendants, who lived down in Attala County, the only other living relatives were Tom's Aunt Iola, who lived back up behind Hebron church with her nephews, West and Weir, bachelors and retired schoolteachers, now in their sixties and almost as addled as their Aunt Iola.

Of course there was Camilla. And Kiki. Ouida had forgotten to ask Old Man Goodwin if Kiki had any children. What on earth would she do if Kiki showed up with a bunch of children? She should have asked Old Man Goodwin about that. He certainly seemed to know a lot more about Kiki than he was telling.

"Mama?"

"We don't have the slightest idea how many to cook for," she said, turned, and went back into the house.

6

Are They Crazy or What

When Ouida had been gone but a few minutes, Hazel craned her neck around the white square column to where she could see Camilla sitting in the swing. "Bud is your mama's only living son," she said, as if she had been reading Ouida's mind.

"It must of really taxed your brain to figure that one out."

"You are hateful. You know that?"

"And mean, too. Bet I'm the meanest girl in the whole state of Mississippi."

"That's something I wouldn't be so proud of if I was you."

Camilla looked up. "You know, that is exactly what Perce used to call me. He would say, Camilla Jean, even if you are my little sister, girl, you are mean . . . the meanest girl in the whole state of Mississippi."

"Why would he want to say something like that?"

"Because I used to pester the hell out of him. And I was always doing something I wasn't supposed to. Like that one time he caught me smoking a cigar I stole out of the store. It was the day before he left for the last time. He was home on furlough. Every time I bothered him or something, he would say the exact same words about me being mean. Lord, I remember it like it was yesterday, the last time he was home alive. Exactly four years ago come next Friday. It was the week school was out—that's how come I remember it so exactly. You know what I can't see for the life of me?"

"What?"

"I swear I can't see why you are sitting there on those old dirty steps like you are doing, with that beautiful chiffon dress. If I was you I'd pull it off and hang it up so it'd be fresh for the funeral tomorrow. Boy, if I had me a chiffon dress like that one, you wouldn't catch me sitting there on no damned dirty ole steps getting the tail of it as black as Lavina's face."

"I'll thank you to leave the tail of my dress and Lavina's black face out of your conversations, if you please."

"Well pin a rose on you. Just sit there and get it dirty, and see if I care. Next time you wear that dress, people are going to think you messed in your panties."

"I do not like that reference," Hazel said quickly. "And I wouldn't be talking about how a person was dressed, if I was you."

"Suit yourself, but those steps are dirtier than all hell, and I guess I know because I'm the one that didn't sweep them since we heard they were bringing Perce home. Lavina said it was bad luck."

"What are you talking about?"

"Lavina said it was bad luck to sweep the front steps while a body was in the house, until it was carried out again, or even after you found out they were bringing a body in the house. I guess you can sweep the back ones all you want to, but not the front ones. Ain't that funny?"

"It's not one bit funny. It ain't a thing but some crazy nigger notion," Hazel said. "Besides, it is my dress, and I can get it dirty if I want to, and I don't see where it is any of your business," Hazel said. "This is terrible—I could just murder Bud Kantwith."

"Be my guest."

"You wouldn't think you were so smart if you were the one's been in Chicago all winter saving up money for a trip to Florida just once, come the month of May, and have this funeral mess come up. All I've thought about since we've lived in Chicago is going to Florida just once. So I buy a bunch of new clothes for my trip, and where do I wind up? At a funeral. And then we're not here five minutes and Bud just runs off and leaves me sitting here," she whined.

"I don't see what you'd want to go to Florida for anyway. Hell, it wasn't twenty minutes ago you were bitching about how hot it is here, and it gets a damned lot hotter in Florida. Anybody can tell you that."

"Naturally *you* are missing the point entirely."

"If you want to know the truth, I was surprised to see you all driving up here this morning. I didn't think you'd come."

"How come you didn't think we'd come?" Hazel asked, craning her neck around the column again.

"Bud and Perce . . . They never were very close, to be brothers. Not that they fought all the time or anything like that. They always acted more like strangers than anything else. When we got the notice that Perce was dead, Bud come home from Memphis for the weekend that same day, and you know he didn't as much as shed a tear when mama told him about Perce. He just tried to cheer her up . . . Boy, she took on most of the night, like she was gonna die. She and Perce were close—I guess that was because he was the oldest. You ever notice it seems like a woman is always closest to her oldest?"

"I don't know. My mama never had no boys."

"Why, the day Perce left for the army, I thought mama was going to have to take to her bed . . . I guess I took it pretty hard too, especially that last time he had to go back. I sure wanted him to take me with him, I swear I did—"

Camilla stared off across Bogue Chitto Bottom for a moment before going on: "He tried to slip off early in the morning, before I woke up, but I was already awake, and I ran and caught up with him right down there by the store, yelling for him to take me with him and carrying on like I was crazy. But he didn't . . . take me with him. I just couldn't understand why he couldn't. Wouldn't that have been funny? I mean, Perce walking into the army camp with his duffel bag in one hand and me hanging on the other? Couldn't you have just seen some old general's face? Perce would have said: 'General, this is my little sister, Camilla, who is mean as hell and has come to the army with me to fight that bunch of North Koreans, or whatever it is you got that has to be fought!' "

She stared at the pan of lima beans she'd shelled and said softly: "I swear he would have, and wouldn't they have just died . . . But he didn't take me. And that was the last time I ever saw him alive—the last time I ever saw him, period, when you think about it . . . I wonder when they are going to get here with him?"

"Ha!"

"Ha, what?"

"From what I hear, they just dig up any old body and send it back. You don't even know for sure it is really your brother they're bringing back. It could be some stranger," Hazel said.

"That's awful."

"What difference does it make?"

"Well, I guess it makes one hell of a lot of difference to know if it is your brother or some perfect stranger you're crying over and burying. How would you like it if we went to the trouble of burying some stranger?" Camilla asked.

"Personally, I couldn't care less."

"Well, I don't think I would appreciate the humor of it none, to go to all that trouble of having a funeral for some perfect stranger. You know, that is one thing really getting mama where it hurts—somebody told her that too—not knowing for sure if it's Perce who's gonna be in that coffin. Tom, too. You'd think they could open it up at the funeral home and look—"

"They wouldn't find nothing but somebody's bones."

"I guess so. You know what would be really strange?"

"What?" Hazel replied, without interest.

"What if they really did get somebody else mixed up with Perce and sent the wrong one? You know, Lavina's sister had a boy that got killed in Korea, too? What if they sent her boy for Perce and Perce for him? Wouldn't that be damned weird? Perce winding up buried in some colored graveyard and us burying Lavina's nephew over yonder at Hebron in the middle of a bunch of Kantwiths? But I don't guess it'd make a damn bit of difference to them, even if that did happen. They are dead. I wonder what it feels like to be dead?"

"I don't know. I'm sure I don't care."

"You would if you were the one's dead. You know there used to be this old woman named Mrs. Duckett that lived back over toward Wardsville, down toward the Natchez Trace, that used to come and visit my Grannie Kantwith all the time when I was a little girl, and all that old woman ever talked about was about people she knew about who had been buried alive. She must of known about a hundred cases of people who were put in their graves alive and then woke up and found themselves buried—"

"Are you crazy? How would she know about it, if people were buried and still alive?" Hazel asked incredulously.

"I don't know, but that is all that old woman ever talked about. I think it was because she belonged to some church that didn't believe in embalming people before they buried them—"

"That still don't make any *sense*. How would she know if they'd been buried alive unless somebody dug them up to see?"

"I don't know how she knew. All I know is, she was about half crazy on the subject, and that was all she ever talked about—"

"She must of been plumb crazy."

"Maybe she was, but you know what she made her husband and two sons promise her when she got sick and knew she was going to die?"

"I hope she made them promise to embalm her like decent folks do, is what I hope."

"Nope. She made them promise they'd cut a hole in her coffin and run a pipe down in it, and listen to it for a couple of days, so if she woke up they could dig her up while she was still alive."

"Good God in Heaven. Did they do it?"

"Yep."

"Well, what happened? Did she wake up?"

"Nope. The next day somebody went back over there to that old country cemetery to see if they'd heard anything out of that pipe, and there wasn't even anybody there listening—"

"That just proves that somebody had more sense than she did."

"That's not the half of it. It was all wet around where that pipe come up out of the ground. Somebody had gone down to the spring and hauled up enough water to fill that pipe clean up to the top!"

"You know what?" Hazel said, looking around the post again. "I don't believe one word of that story, and I think you are just about the lyingest person I ever met in my life!"

"Well, you better believe it, 'cause it's true. I happened to know that ole Mrs. Duckett personally and heard her carry on about them buried alive folks a hundred times," Lavina said, opening the screen door. "Camilla, you got them butterbeans shelled yet?"

"Well then, how come they'd go and fill that pipe and everything up with water like that?" Hazel asked.

"Maybe because they got sick and tired of hearing that ole woman carrying on about folks being buried alive and was making sure she stayed where she was at," Lavina answered. She took the shelled beans and went back into the house.

"That's plain disgusting," Hazel said, then waited until she was sure Lavina was out of earshot. "In Chicago we don't let our colored cleaning women get familiar enough to address us on a first name basis."

"Lavina is not a cleaning woman," Camilla replied. "She keeps the house, and she's like family."

"Maybe your family . . . How come you're not in school, you said?"

"I got excused. I went into Mr. Burden's office—he's the principal—and asked if I could have tomorrow off for the funeral, and he said I could and to take today off, too. Did you bring another dress with you to wear to the funeral?"

"Yes."

"Is it as pretty as that one?"

"No. It ain't chiffon. It ain't proper to wear chiffon to a funeral. Even for a man's been dead two years."

"Today is . . . You know I am in this contest at school? It's to pick the May Queen they have every year. The May Queen is the person who will be the queen of the spring dance, which is the only dance they have at that old school, unless you count the tacky old things they have after the home football games—"

"So good luck."

"Ha. There's three other girls in the contest all coming in ahead of me, you'd better believe. The way they do it is, each class in high school elects one girl to be their candidate, and I was elected the one from the senior class. That is sort of an honor in itself. When you get elected by secret ballot by your class, it makes you feel good, even if you know you ain't got a snowball in hell chance of getting elected May Queen. There is a running argument which is better, to get elected Homecoming Queen by the football team or Miss Bolatusha High School by the student body or May Queen. Alice Jones got herself elected to both those other honors and would of won May Queen hands down too, if the senior class had picked her for their candidate instead of me, and don't you think she's letting them forget about that for one minute. Boy, you never saw such a stuck up bitch in your life. Now she's going around telling everybody how they should elect Jeanie Downs, even if she is just a freshman, and not to vote for me. And those other girls in the contest all have folks who will stick fistfuls of money in old jugs. Ain't that a crappy way to elect a queen? They got some old gallon jugs with your name and picture stuck on them, and people put money in them for votes—a penny a vote—and the one that ends up with the most money by nine o'clock tonight wins. Fat chance I got of winning, since I won't even be there. Tonight's when she gets elected."

"When who gets elected?" Hazel asked.

"The May Queen. Weren't you listening? They got this fund raising carnival for the new gym, and the girl that ends up with the most money tonight will get crowned May Queen at the dance Saturday night. I can't be there, which is just one more reason I won't get elected, but I will be one of the maids anyway . . . At least that is something. It's the first thing I've ever been since I've been going to that old school."

"I just wish Bud would get his butt on back here. That is what I wish."

"I guess it's just as well I can't go. It will save me the embarrassment of coming in last. Hell, mama would give birth to a litter of rabbits if I even acted like I wanted to go, with Perce's funeral tomorrow. Besides, the only thing I got to wear that is even half formal is that old blue net dress I made in home ec class, and it don't look very good on me . . . blue just ain't my color. Come to think about it, I look more like a clown than a queen in that old thing. I don't know why mama let ole Buford Jones sell her that old blue material. Likely Alice was there and sold it to her, the bitch she is. I look good in yellow though . . . You don't know how lucky you are, being able to buy pretty clothes like that dress. You know, I have never had a scrap of chiffon on me in my life?"

"Don't think that makes you something special," Hazel said, getting up from the steps and finding more shade in one of the white wooden chairs on the other side of the porch from Camilla. "I don't see why you're so worried about not having anything to wear to this function, if you ain't going in the first place. And if you're hinting for me to loan you my dress, you may as well get that thought right out of your head. I don't lend my clothes."

"I was not! I wouldn't be caught dead in one of your *frocks*!"

"Good. Because—" Hazel stopped speaking, open mouthed and staring at the three people standing at the foot of the steps. Neither of them had noticed the old people walk up. They were two men in their late sixties who appeared as if they could be twins and, between them, a very old woman who was shielding her face with a large old cloth purse, which she held by its wooden handle. Camilla got up and greeted them.

"Aunt Iola. You all come on in. Mama is in the house someplace. How are you, Cousin West?" She asked. She knew there was no point in speaking to Cousin Weir, as he never spoke back anyway. "Do you all remember Hazel? Bud's wife?" she asked, as the men helped the old woman up the steps.

"Who did you say she was? Some of Ouida's kin?" the old woman, like many old people gone deaf, shouted, still shielding her face with the purse.

"No," Camilla shouted back. "She's my brother's wife. Bud, you know?"

"Is he the one they're burying?" she asked of one of the men.

"No, Aunt Iola. That's the oldest. He'd be the other boy. The one they had to keep back in school," West replied.

"There's no excuse for that," the old woman shouted. "Somebody ought to take a barrel stave to him." And with that, she entered the house, as Cousin West held the door open for her. He then nodded at Hazel and followed Weir inside.

"I never met them folks in my life," Hazel said. "Who are they?"

"Oh, I thought you met them that first time Bud brought you home," Camilla answered.

"Well, there was a whole mob of people here, but I don't think I remember them. Are they some of your kin?"

"Yep. West and Weir are Tom's first cousins, and Iola is his aunt. There used to be three of them."

"Three of what . . . ? And how come she kept her old purse in front of her face like that?"

"Three old aunts—Iola was the youngest, and then there was Iwilla, who was West and Weir's mama, and then Inez, who was the oldest. They were all schoolteachers, but Iwilla was the only one that ever got married. To some man she met, taught at Milsaps in Jackson. That was how she had West and Weir."

"Well are they crazy or what? That old woman kept that old purse in front of her face the whole time, and that one old man didn't as much as look at me—"

"They're crazier than hell, if you want to know the truth. Sometimes when you go over to their house—they live right over yonder up past Hebron Church. You can see the top of their house if you look hard enough from this end of the porch—"

"No thanks. I'm not standing in that hot sun trying to see nobody who's crazy's house—"

"You can see it real plain in the winter. Anyway, if you go over there sometimes, Aunt Iola will sit there in the kitchen with a paper sack over her head the whole time you're there—"

"She'll do *what*?"

"Sit there the whole time with a paper sack over her head. Or sometimes she'll hide in the pantry and talk to you through a crack in the door. She doesn't like to look at people. Weir doesn't either, but he also doesn't like to talk to anyone he doesn't know. He braids rag rugs. Sometimes he'll stay up all night braiding on one by lamplight. Aunt Iola won't let them have electricity in the house, because she's afraid lightning will come in on the wires and blow up the house."

"Well, I know I never saw them before. I'd remember seeing that bunch."

"Probably not. Now that I think about it, they probably didn't come down here that first time Bud brought you home and we had that picnic. They don't like to go around a bunch of strangers, although I did sort of expect them to show up here today. About the only place they ever go is to funerals. They can even get Aunt Iola to get into that old car of West's, if it is to go to a funeral, and he's run the damn thing in Bogue Chitto Creek about three times. Once they were on their way to a funeral up close to Huntsville, and he sailed that thing right off a bridge into Poplar Creek during spring high water. And you know that old car just floated right on down the creek and ended up in somebody's pasture. And they just sat there and waited until somebody came and pulled them out, with Aunt Iola keeping her head covered up with a shawl the whole time—"

"I never heard of anybody so crazy in my life. I'm sure glad they're not kin to me."

"Oh?"

"What do you mean, oh?"

"They're pretty close kin to Bud."

"I'm not ignorant. I guess I figured that out."

Camilla didn't say anything. But she did giggle.

"What is it you find so funny? If I had a bunch of crazy folks like that kin to me, I don't think I would find it all that funny."

"Bet you won't find it all that funny when you figure out how close kin those folks are going to be to your baby either, will you?"

"What?"

"Oh, hell, I wouldn't worry too much about it, if I were you. Not all the Kantwiths are crazy. But it sure seems to have a way of cropping up pretty often. To be honest with you, I think I'm the only living Kantwith who is not either crazy or too damned dumb to come in out of the rain. Of course there is Aunt Kiki. We don't know about her . . . What's the matter with you? You feeling sick or something?" Camilla asked, as Hazel got up and rushed into the house.

7

Twice, Slowly, Around The Courthouse Square

Being another Kantwith that was not either crazy or too dumb to come in out of the rain, Katherine Chislom, when she caught up with what appeared to be a small funeral procession on the highway between Winona and Bolatusha, had the good sense to slow down and avoid drawing any excess attention to herself and the custom made Cadillac she was driving.

When the hearse turned at the red light onto Yates Street, which would carry it down Bolatusha's main street, she continued on the highway that looped around downtown, to Harvey's Standard Station and Cafe, and the junction of the county road that ran southward to Kantwith and on through the old town of Wardsville, before crossing the Natchez Trace and eventually joining the state highway between Kosciusko and Ackerman.

Bud Kantwith and Bevo Harvey were just getting into Bud's car, parked in front of the cafe, when Katherine pulled up to the service island and stopped. As Bud backed up the car and executed a U-turn that would take them back in the direction of downtown Bolatusha, Bevo spied the woman getting out of the maroon colored Cadillac. "Did you *see* that?" he asked.

"See what?" Bud was watching for traffic before pulling out into the highway.

"That woman. Looks like some goddamn movie star getting out of that tailor made Caddy."

Bud looked in the rear view mirror and got a quick glance at the tall, slender woman, as she walked around the front of the car.

"I'd give my left nut for a piece of that," Bevo said.

"And your right one for that Caddy. Then where would you be?" Bud asked, as he pulled out into the highway.

"You wouldn't want to know. It's got Texas tags," Bevo said, still looking back.

"Somebody just passing through is all," Bud said.

"Don't many like that pass through Bolatusha, and I ought to know 'cause I see most of what passes through here."

Three hundred yards down the highway, Bud turned left and picked up Main Street at its south end. Near the downtown courthouse square they came upon the hearse, followed by Tom's car and three or four others, including that of the Sheriff, Matt McNeil, who pulled in behind the procession as it entered the square.

"That's your brother . . . That's Perce they're bringing in!" Bevo said.

"How come they're going so slow?" Bud asked, having slowed down himself as he came abreast of the hearse and, seeing Tom's car, began blowing his horn to attract his father's attention.

"Well, goddamn, Bud."

Dennis Thomson, a young man who paid attention to what was what, was doing his damnedest to keep the speedometer at a steady fifteen miles an hour, as he made a circle around the square and then another just as his father had instructed him to do. Perce Kantwith was the only soldier from Bogue Chitto that had been killed in the Korean War, as Boswell Thomson had pointed out to him, if you didn't count the Kent boy, whose wife had buried him in San Diego, California, and the two Negro boys from over around Wardsville. And their funerals were being handled by the colored undertaking parlor from Kosciusko. Dennis, only three months home from mortician's college in Birmingham, realized that his father had put a lot of trust in him, letting him drive the new hearse through Bolatusha with what could be said to be Bogue Chitto's only war hero to come out of the recent conflict.

And then that goddamn Bud Kantwith had to come along blowing his car horn like it was a BHS homecoming parade instead of something in honor of his own brother. Well, his father had always said that anybody who ever tried to figure out that Kantwith bunch would end up crazy themselves, and if anybody knew it, he did.

"Hot in that wool suit, huh?" Dennis said to the young soldier sitting beside him, as he nodded hello in the direction of Old Man Goodwin, who was standing in front of the bank. The soldier nodded that, yes, it was hot, and Dennis was glad that he wasn't in the army and didn't have to go around wearing wool suits escorting bodies in this kind of weather. It had to be getting on close to ninety degrees. "Where did you say it was you're from?"

"California," the soldier, whose name was James Lyon Hansen, replied.

"Los Angles, huh?" Dennis Thomson asked. That, Hollywood, and San Francisco were the only places he knew the names of in California. Oh, and San Diego, where they had buried the Kent boy.

"Santa Barbara," the soldier replied.

"Oh. Is that close to Hollywood?"

"No. Up the coast. Between Los Angeles and San Francisco."

"Oh, yeah," Dennis Thomson said and waved at old Miss Maybelle Duke, who taught history at the high school and was standing on the corner with a bunch of other old ladies waving little American flags they'd bought at Newberry's. It was lunch hour, and the street was lined with teachers and students from the high school.

Actually, James Lyon Hansen was from Solvang, a Danish village near Santa Barbara, but he was quite sure he'd find himself involved in a web of explanations if he mentioned it. And as pleasant as young Thomson was trying to be, it was just too damned hot to be explaining anything about a place that compared to Bolatusha about as much as some village in Korea. He couldn't ever remember being so hot, and wondered why the army didn't give him summer issue for this trip. And on top of the heat, he didn't have the slightest idea where he was going or what he'd find when he got there. This was only his second funeral detail, but he'd heard some pretty weird stories about some of the families from other guys who'd pulled this duty.

And when they came back to the highway, which obviously looped around the business section of the little town, then turned onto a gravel road after they'd gone but a short distance, right near a big Standard Oil sign, his fears worsened. The hill they were traveling down, picking up speed, ran straight for a couple of miles. Beyond, it looked like a wilderness. He'd heard too many stories about southern backwoods to feel comfortable.

Old Man Goodwin was not, at that moment, feeling very comfortable either. Katherine Chislom had just walked through the door of the bank and, without breaking stride, was headed directly to the rear and the semi-private corner where his desk was located. He managed to keep from wiping the palms of his hands on his pants as he got up to greet her.

"Good morning, Donald," she said, extending one hand in his direction and swinging a large leather bag from her shoulder with the other. "Shall we go into your father's office?" A mischievous grin played at her mouth as she glanced around the bank. "Or, we can conduct our business here, if you prefer."

"No, no. My father's office . . ." His eyes followed hers around the bank. All business had come to a halt, and all eyes, those of the four employees and three customers, were on Katherine. None of the people working in the bank would know her, except for Miss Black, and she only by name. Of the customers, well, old Mr. Shelbyville Pickett had trouble enough just remembering his own grandchildren, at his age. Of course, Mrs. Beth Ward was certainly taking it all in, but even if she did recognize Kiki, she had the closest mouth in all of Bogue Chitto.

"Why haven't you ever moved in here?" Katherine asked, as he followed her into his father's office and closed the door.

"I guess I've gotten used to being where I can see everything. Besides," he laughed nervously, "maybe I've been saving it for you. You all but own the bank now."

"In name only, Donald. I have no intention of interfering with your operation of the bank's business. Except, of course, where certain land holdings and mineral rights are concerned—"

"And investments of the bank's assets. And I couldn't welcome that more. Sit down . . . sit down," Donald said, pulling his father's chair out from the large old glass-covered desk. "How was your trip?"

"Thank you," she said, taking a file folder from the leather bag as she sat down. "My trip? Long and boring. I had to come through Dallas, and by the time I was halfway through Arkansas,

I was beginning to wish I'd flown to Jackson and bought a car there. Now, all the contracts are here and in order. You'll find my signature on each of them and witnessed by my lawyers, who, by the way, think I could find much better things to do with my money than buy up the controlling stock of a little counry bank."

"But a profitable one," Donald quickly pointed out.

"Yes. As I told you when you were last in Houston—and have now made official—you will have a free hand in the day-to-day operations of the bank, as you've had in the past. And, of course, as your father did. Except, of course, where land transactions involving my brother are concerned. There will be no more of that sort of thing—"

"For which Miss Ouida will be eternally grateful, I suspect."

"Ouida?"

"Yes. I don't think you realize what a teribble burden he has placed on her. On his family."

"On the contrary. I think I do realize that. Your father sent me detailed reports that included the particulars of a rather sordid—"

"Yes. Of course," Donald Goodwin said quickly, and felt his face going red.

Kiki laughed. "Your problem, Donald, is that you're just too damned decent. I've sort of missed those gossipy little footnotes your father used to send. Is Tom still spending Saturday nights with Mavis Patton?"

Donald nodded, his face turning a beet red.

"How old would she be now?"

"About forty-seven. Tom's age." he answered.

"It's a wonder to me that Ouida didn't divorce him years ago."

"Women like Miss Ouida don't get divorces."

"No. I suppose they don't. Has Tom attempted to buy anything since I last spoke to you?"

"He had an appointment with me this morning, in regards to the old Crenshaw place—"

"Where is that?"

"Over the other side of Poplar Creek. Up toward the Choctaw County line," Donald replied.

"Somewhat out of the area of our interest. But he wouldn't know that, of course?" Kiki said, all business now.

"Of course. Surely you don't think I—"

"No, I don't think you'd tell him, as it wouldn't be in your best interest to do so. With our agreement now official, you stand a chance of becoming a very rich man off the property my dear brother has been willy-nilly purchasing with my money the last six years. Not nearly as much as it would have been if he'd known what he was doing. However your father was quite astute in keeping him from making a complete fool of himself. A major portion of the land should prove to be worth . . . who knows? At least it should turn a very neat profit in a few years and the rest, as you've pointed out, can be disposed of without our suffering a loss we can't absorb in tax write-offs. So there we have it. Or perhaps I should say, you have it, now."

"Yes . . .," Donald said, lighting a cigarette. His hands were shaking, and he felt sweaty. His bout of nerves came not from what Katherine was saying but from what she *wasn't* saying. She could pull the plug on him, as well as on her brother, anytime she took the notion.

She looked at him and smiled, and he felt as if she was reading his mind. "What happened in regard to the Crenshaw farm?" she asked.

"Nothing happened."

"You surely didn't let him buy it?"

"No. I didn't keep the appointment. I suspect he'll be back in here looking for me before long."

"*You* didn't keep an appointment? I find that hard to believe, Donald. You always keep your appointments."

"Not this one," he said and sat down in the chair across from her. "Kiki—"

"Kiki! You haven't called me that since—"

"I'm sorry—"

"Be my guest. I suppose I'd better get used to it."

"Katherine, there is something I feel I have to tell you—"

"Surely you didn't lose your nerve and tell Tom?"

"No."

"The peace warrant. You didn't get the peace warrant?"

"I got it, and Matt McNeil will be serving it today—after Perce's home. I still don't know why you need a peace warrant to protect a grave in Hebron cemetery from your brother."

"Not *a* grave. The grave of my son. Surely your father told you about my son?"

"Some. Not everything. And he didn't tell me anything about it until he realized he was dying. I'd always heard—or assumed—you'd had a miscarriage."

Katherine's face went hard, and Donald Goodwin became the second person that day to make a mental note to remind himself never to cross her. "Not exactly a miscarriage, Donald. I was in my seventh month when I had my baby. My *seventh* month. He was fully formed. Perfect. He could have lived. He would have lived . . ."

"I'm sorry. I don't know everything . . ."

"There is no everything for you to know."

"The grave has been there all these years—"

"I know exactly how many years, how many months, how many weeks, and how many days the grave has been there, unmarked, untended—"

"No, Katherine—"

"But no more. The people from Kosciusko Stone Monument are putting a stone on my son's grave today. It will read "Michael, infant son of Katherine Kantwith. Born August 6, 1942, murdered August 6, 1942—"

"Jesus, God!"

"The world will know that unmarked grave in the back corner of Hebron churchyard is that of my son, and—"

"*Today*?"

"Today."

He took a deep breath. "In that case, I don't feel that I have to apologize for what I'm going to tell you. And if it angers you . . . If you feel you are justified in taking a course of action that may affect our partnership in any way, then . . . Then I'll live with it."

"What on earth are you talking about, Donald?" she asked, her face again going as cold as the marble she'd find on her son's grave.

"Katherine, the grave of your son has not gone unmarked all these years. Nor has it gone untended. There is a small marker on the grave. I didn't realize until you reminded me last week, when you called about my getting the warrant—" Donald stopped and collected his words:

"My father only told me that you'd had a baby that night you were brought to him. I didn't think any more about it until you reminded me last week. About where your baby might have been buried. I would certainly never have thought it would be in Hebron—"

"It was done very quietly and very early in the morning. Boswell Thomson took the casket out there in the back seat of his car, and Tom made sure there was no one around. Not, certainly, out of any concern for me or my baby, but to protect his own ass. Of course Boswell never said anything. Your father, I understand, loaned Boswell the money to buy his business. Some fool once said that money talks. Well, I've never seen it talk but I've certainly seen it buy a lot of silence."

"Yes," Donald said, thoughtfully. "Then the best sort of silence is given freely as a gift."

"What are you talking about?"

"Miss Ouida. And the grave of your child."

"Yes?"

"I went out there after I talked to you. Boswell told me where to find the grave. There is a plain little cross about a foot high marking your baby's grave, Katherine. And it has not been untended. There are flowers planted on that grave. Annuals, planted this year—"

"Who?"

"Miss Ouida, of course."

"Or Lavina. She was there. Ouida was away visiting her parents with the children when it happened," Katherine said.

"No, Katherine. Lavina, too, perhaps. But not Lavina without Miss Ouida. You know that."

"Yes," she admitted. "I suppose I do. Ouida was always the soul of kindness."

"I'm glad you realize that. Then you'll understand why I had to tell her, I hope."

"You told her what?"

"That you were coming here today. Let your arrival be a surprise or a shock, or whatever you plan it to be, to Tom. But I couldn't let you do that to Miss Ouida. She's a kind, good woman who has suffered enough."

"She'll tell Tom. Surely she'll tell Tom."

"No. She won't tell him. And Camilla won't either. I'd bet what interest I have left in this bank on that."

"Camilla? The little girl?"

"She's not a little girl anymore, Katherine. She's almost grown, graduating from high school next week. She's smart, I hear. Heading up her class."

"Is she pretty?"

"Pretty enough. Not like you were—"

Katherine laughed, and Old Man Goodwin relaxed. "I'm not pretty anymore? Is that what you're saying, Donald?"

"That is not what I meant, and you know it. She just didn't get the Kantwith looks. Perce was the only one of Tom's children who did . . . I just couldn't let you show up there this day without warning Miss Ouida."

"I understand."

"I don't know if you do or not, Katherine. That woman has been put through hell and back. And from what I understand, the daughter . . . Well, it's gossip, but I hear Tom's trying to marry her off to Joiner Whittal's boy."

"Joiner Whittal? Is he still alive?"

"Barely. He's got cancer."

"Great God. Did you know that Tom tried to marry *me* off to Joiner Whittal after his wife died? You wouldn't know that unless your father told you. You were in the army at the time. And he's still trying to get a slice of old Joiner's pie through the females in his family. Someone should shoot Tom Kantwith."

"Seriously, I hope that is not what you have in mind."

"Don't be silly. I'm not going to let him off that easy."

"But you're going out there?"

"Of course. I didn't drive all the way from Houston just to bring you those contracts." She glanced at her watch. "However, I really don't think I should arrive so soon after the body—"

"What am I thinking of? Gene made me promise I'd bring you home to dinner if you got here by noon!"

"Are you sure? Of course, I really would like to see her again."

"Of course I'm sure," he said, standing. "And I'd just as soon Tom not find you here, when he comes storming in to find out why I didn't keep this mornin's appointment. He's got a temper," he added, taking Katherine by the arm.

"I should know that better than anyone. This time, however, he's not dealing with a defenseless little college kid."

"No, indeed he's not. I hope you like chicken and dressing. That's what Gene said she was going to fix."

"Love it. We'll take my car."

"It will be my pleasure to be chauffeured by you, Mrs. Chislom," Old Man Goodwin replied.

Mrs. Beth Ward was standing outside the bank. She caught Donald's eye and winked. He wondered why.

8

I Know And You Know, But Does He Know?

Camilla was still sitting in the swing when Ouida came out on the porch again, followed by Lavina.

"Come on in and eat some dinner before they get here," Ouida said. "And I'm telling you the last time to take off them shorts and put on a decent dress. Hazel said you wanted to borrow one of her dresses. Haven't you got dresses of your own to put on?"

Camilla glanced at Lavina before answering. "Hazel has got a big mouth on her."

"Well, go have your dinner. It's on the table, and Lavina has to take something down to her house for Henry to eat."

"Henry can forge for himself. I'm staying right here with you until them folks get here with Perce's body."

"Are you going to just sit there, or are you going to pay attention to me?" Ouida asked.

"You better go eat, girl. You gonna make yourself sick, you didn't have breakfast on top of it."

"If I ate anything, I think I would throw up. Lavina, what? Where do you think Jamie boy got off to?"

"Never you mind about Jamie Boy. It's you we're talking about right now," she answered. "Besides, when I go home I'm gonna send Henry off looking for him."

Camilla looked at Ouida: "Did you tell her about Aunt Kiki?"

"I told her."

"Been me I'd ask that Old Man Goodwin where she's coming *from*? Ain't a soul I know of heard a word from her since way back yonder in that war they had, and then him coming out here just like that, says she's coming home? Been a dozen years, and how come the banker's the one to come out here telling it? Something about this ain't right. Except—" Lavina quickly shut her mouth, having, in her own mind, found the connecting thread between young Old Man Goodwin and Kiki Kantwith. She had never told anyone, not even Ouida, about her own role—and that Henry played—in the events of that August night and day so long ago. Too, as she had often told Henry over the years, the least that Kiki Kantwith could do was let her know something about how she was doing; if she was well, happy, even alive. But no—

"Except what? Camilla asked.

"Except what what?" Lavina asked.

"You were saying 'something about this ain't right.' Then you said, 'except.' Except what?"

"Except nothing. I lost my thoughts."

Camilla looked at her. She knew that Lavina was lying. She also knew that Lavina would never tell her about what, until she took a notion to do so. If she ever did.

Ouida quickly changed the subject: "What made Hazel think you wanted to borrow one of her dresses? For the funeral?"

"No'm. We were talking about the fund raising carnival at the school tonight, and I just happened to mention I didn't have anything at all to wear, and she blew a gasket thinking I was asking her to borrow that old yellow dress she's got on."

"Have you gone crazy even thinking about going off to a carnival with your brother's body lying in the front parlor like it'll be?"

"Mama, it is not a real carnival. They just call it that."

"Well, be quiet about it. I don't care what they call it, you're not going, and that's all there is to it. I would have thought you'd have the decency not to mention it to me with Perce's funeral and all. Now go in the house with Lavina and eat something before you make yourself sick."

"If you can stand to eat at the table with them old men," Lavina said. "I swear them old men always put my nose in mind of wet puppies, the way they smell—"

"Mama . . . Mama . . . *Mama*!

"What? What is the matter with you?"

Camilla stood and pointed. "It's them, It's Thomson's hearse."

"Oh, Lord! I don't know . . . I just don't know . . . Camilla, where is your brother, Bud? I don't know what to do. The Lord knows I been looking forward to this day nigh on to two years, and now it has come, and I just don't know what to do . . . what to do—"

"Now, Miz Ouida, you get hold of yourself," Lavina said, putting her arm around the woman. "Now you just got to be strong and take hold of yourself."

"They're driving slow . . . like they ought to with the dead," Ouida said quietly.

"That's Bud's car in back . . . and the Sheriff, too. I didn't expect the Sheriff would come out here with them" Camilla said.

"What is it?" Hazel asked, coming out onto the porch.

"They're coming," Camilla answered.

"That's our car. Bud must of met up with them."

"And would you look who else? Who's riding with Tom Kantwith? Progress Whittal," Camilla said, angrily. "I don't know what made him think he had to go and stick his nose in this—"

"Camilla," Lavina said, and nodded at Ouida, who glanced to the hearse and quickly away, like a thing trapped and smelling it's own fear.

"What should I do?" Ouida asked. "I don't know what I should do . . ."

"Don't do nothing, Miz Ouida. Just steady yourself."

The four women stood on the porch, none of them moving, until the hearse pulled into the yard and stopped. Then Ouida slowly made her way down the steps, shrugging off Lavina's helping hand.

"Perce? My Perce? Come home at last? Oh, my Lord, my baby Perce," she said, as she slowly walked toward the hearse. Dennis Thomson and James Lyon Hansen opened the doors and got out, then stopped to watch the keening woman walking towards them.

"Mama?" Camilla said, and looked at Lavina. "What can I do?"

"Nothing, child. Just go steady her. I'm going on down to my house," she answered, turning back toward the front door.

"Perce? My baby, Perce . . . ? Perce! Perce! What did he ever do? Look at it here!"

Matt McNeil opened his car door and got out, saw Ouida, and quickly turned away, too embarrassed to watch. Warrant or no warrant, he made up his mind that, the moment he paid his respects to Miss Ouida, he was getting back in his car and driving straight back to town. Peace warrants that made no sense in the first place could wait their own good time.

"Mama. Now mama. Don't take on so," Camilla said, taking Ouida by the hand. "Mama—"

"Walked off this hill smiling and full of life, and now he's come home in a box in that old hot hearse—"

Ouida began sobbing and turned her head to Camilla's arms just as Progress Whittal walked over and put his hand on her shoulder, drawn by a grief that was not his, but one that he wanted to share. Camilla reacted to the sensation of his fingers on her bare flesh as if she'd been touched by ice cubes. She turned to Progress with a fury in her eyes, and spat through clenched teeth: "Progress, you get your goddamn hand off me, and you turn your butt around and head off this hill, if you know what's good for you. You hear me?"

"I just—"

"No just anything. Move!"

Progress backed off, glanced at Dennis Thomson and the soldier, and knew they'd heard. He wished he could hide. Or had not listened to Tom Kantwith when he'd insisted at the bank that he ride out here with him. The way Camilla acted sometimes, he had to wonder if Tom was telling the truth when he said that she looked with favor on his attentions.

Lavina, who had stopped to watch through the screen door, suppressed a grin. Nobody had to tell *her* what Camilla had said. She walked through the house to the kitchen, and only paused long enough to pick up the basket with Henry's dinner in it and went on, never glancing at the three old people at the table or telling them to help themselves as she normally would have done.

Henry was frying some eggs when she arrived in her own kitchen. "Throw that mess out to the dogs," she said. "I got some chicken and Irish potato salad and a piece of Miz Ouida's devil food cake she made yesterday. Soon's you eat I want you to get on the road looking for Jamie. Not back by now, something's happened to him."

"You ask Tom Kantwith what happened to my boy?" Henry asked, seating himself at the table. "Ain't nothing ever happen around here Tom Kantwith don't know about."

Lavina stared at her husband for a moment before answering back. "You know, for once I think there's something he don't know. I don't think he knows what happened to Jamie."

"What makes you say that?"

"I can read Tom Kantwith better'n a book. That's what makes me think that. This morning when I went in that kitchen, and he was sitting there by the window and looked at me, I would of known. Sooner or later he'll know, but right now I don't think he knows any more than we know."

"Well, I don't know if I can rightfully believe that to be the truth."

"Well there's one man who would know, if anybody would. Trace McCall."

"You know I ain't spoke to Trace in ten years."

"Besides the fact. You go and find my boy and bring him home, you hear?" Lavina said, and went to toss the scorched eggs out the back door to the dogs.

"I'll have to walk or catch a ride. You know I can't get that old car started."

"Ain't a soul except Jamie been able to get that old car started for a year now. Soon's he gets home and offers me the explanation of whereabouts he's been, I'm gonna have him start it and drive it to town and have it fixed once and for all."

"Cost money. And he ain't got no leave to drive."

"Leave or no leave. I don't guess Matt McNeill is gonna put him in jail for driving it to Mr. Harvey's station. I got to get back up yonder. On top of everything else, I got them three old folks on my hands, plus Camilla acting plumb crazy."

"What's the matter with her now?"

"Perce. He was more like a daddy to her than any she's ever known. They brought the body in."

Henry stopped eating and looked at her, knew what she was trying not to think. But he had already considered that Jamie was dead; had, in fact, come to accept it as fact. To him the unthinkable had already been thought.

"No! It cannot be. It won't be!" Lavina said. She would will such thoughts away.

Such thoughts had crossed Camilla's mind several times that day, and did again as she stood, still, in the front yard, staring at the door where Tom, the Sheriff, Dennis Thomson, Bevo Harvey, and the soldier had carried Perce's coffin, followed by her mother and Boswell Thomson. She was flanked by Bud and Hazel. Progress Whittal had retreated to the car, in spite of the heat.

"I didn't think she'd take it that bad. I mean he's been dead two *years*."

"Hazel, would you just shut up?" Bud asked, without taking his eyes from the door. To tell the truth, he'd been thinking exactly the same thing.

"God. I feel funny," Camilla said.

"I feel sorry for that soldier," Hazel piped. "Having to ride all the way out here with all them old heavy clothes on. He was sweating like a pig."

"He looks nice," Camilla commented.

"I don't personally pay no attention to soldiers," Hazel replied.

"I guess you'll have to pay some attention to this one, since he'll be staying here until after the funeral. It's going to be military, with taps and all."

"That's your mama's problem, him staying here, none of mine. I'd make him stay in a hotel," Hazel replied.

"Where you going to find a hotel? Winona is the closest. Or Kosciusko, maybe. Anyway, Mama wouldn't let him."

"Like I said, that is her problem—"

"Can't the two of you shut up fussing and bickering for just one solid minute? Mama's got enough on her hands as it is," Bud glared at Hazel, turned, and walked toward Tom's car and Progress Whittal.

"I just can't believe he's in there, for the life of me. It just doesn't seem to be true," Camilla said, still staring at the front door.

"Don't be so sure he is in there."

"I don't believe that old story, and you just be quiet about it, you hear me?"

"I've heard that when they have them big battles? That some of them get blown to bits, and they just haul off and throw them all in one big old grave, not paying the first bit of attention to who is who. More'n likely there ain't the first thing in that old coffin but some rocks."

"I don't believe it. Why would anyone go to all the trouble of sending it back if there wasn't anything in it but some rocks?"

"You didn't seem to think it would make much difference a little while ago," Hazel replied. "Somebody once told me they'd seen a box opened up when the army brought it back, and there wasn't a thing in it but a bunch of bones that didn't even look like human bones. Personally I think they ought to open it up and see what exactly is in there."

"Well, they won't. Boswell Thomson would never do something like that, and that soldier they sent along wouldn't let him in the first place."

"Well, it's not my say-so. But if it was, that's what I would do."

"It's not. So why don't you just mind your own business?"

"I was just saying that is what *I* would do. It ain't none of my concern what is in that old coffin," she said, as Matt McNeil came out of the house. He nodded at Camilla and Hazel, and walked over to where Bud was standing talking to Progress. "Ask your daddy to stop by my office and see me for a moment when he comes into town," the Sheriff said and kept walking toward his car.

"Sure will, Matt!" Bud said, too quickly, too eager to please. As Matt got into the county car and turned it around, Bud crossed the lawn to Camilla and Hazel. Progress ambled over after him.

"Hazel, have you met Progress? Progress Joiner. This is my wife, Hazel."

"How do, ma'm," Progress said and turned his attention to Camilla. "I just want you to know that I didn't mean to push in where I wasn't wanted—," he began.

"Look, Progress. Don't you know there are times when people want to be left alone? Or maybe *be* alone? Don't take it personally, but I really don't feel like having company today, okay?" And with that she walked off around the house toward the wisteria arbor.

Progress started following her: "I guess you won't be going to the doings at the high school tonight, will you? I mean, with Perce and all?" She didn't answer, and he followed her a few more steps.

"I just thought I'd ask, is all. I mean if you need anything or need to get someplace or something, I can be counted on. You know that, don't you Camilla? Just say the word. I've talked to your daddy, and he takes kindly to me driving you around if you want to go someplace or anything. I mean, he don't object to me calling on you . . ."

Camilla kept walking, glancing back at the three of them only briefly once. But it was enough to stop Progress from following her.

"Don't pay her no mind, Prog," Bud said. "She's just upset about Perce and all. Now what kind of cattle did you say it was you and your daddy's been buying."

"Brah*man*. Brahman cows. From India."

"Brahman cows. Did you ever hear of that kind of cattle, Hazel?"

Hazel looked at her husband as if he'd lost his mind.

"Naw," Bud continued. "Hazel don't know the first thing about cows. She's a city gal."

"These cows is more disease resistant. And they don't mind the heat as much as other cows. But they're wild son of a guns. We gonna crossbreed them with our domestic stock."

"Is that a fact? Say, I heard from Bevo that you went and bought yourself a big fine new car. Where is that thing?"

"At the dealer garage. For its thousand mile checkup. And I'm getting some seatcovers put on it. You ought to have seatcovers put on the first thing when you get a new car. It saves the seats from getting wore out. I'm getting some of them new clear plastic ones put on it. I rode out here with your daddy. I got to go back and pick up mine."

"Say, I got to take Bevo back to town. You can ride back with us."

"Bud . . ." That was Hazel starting to protest.

"Why not? I got to take old Bevo back."

"Ain't that undertaker going back?" Hazel asked. "Him in his own car, and that boy in the hearse by his self. Seems like there's plenty of rides going toward town—"

"No problem," Bud said, ignoring her. "I'll take you on over there. Why don't you go on in the house and pay your respects to Mama and see if you can't rescue old Bevo?"

"Bud!"

"Go on, Mama would appreciate it, I know. And I need to talk to my wife a minute."

Hazel seethed until Progress was up the steps and inside the house. The minute the screen door slammed behind him, she turned on Bud. "Now just what do you have to drive that fool into town for? I don't see why you have to run around burning up our gas to show off to ever fool in Mississippi."

"Shut up, Hazel. He'll hear you."

"Well, I don't care if he does. I want you to know I don't like none of this one bit. I could of died out here all this time of suffocation, for all you care, Bud Kantwith. And being way out here in the country like this, what if I suddenly starting having my baby? Out here, with you gone off with the car? How would I get to a doctor?"

"Hazel, honey, the baby ain't due—"

"*I* know when my baby is due. After all, don't forget who the one is that's having it. *I'm* the one missing out on the vacation in Florida that I have saved up for out of my own money! I really hope you don't think for one minute that I'm enjoying any part of this. That little sister of yours is just about the most smart aleck thing I have ever seen in my entire life. It's bad enough you leaving me out here, to die for all you care, without having to put up with the likes of that little bitch on top of it."

"Now, Hazel, you just behave yourself. You want my daddy to hear you talking like that?"

"I don't care who hears me . . . I don't see nobody around here doing nothing for me to write home about—"

"You just try to get along. That's all I ask."

"I don't see why, for Christ's sake. And your mama is just as stuck up as she can be. On top of which, no human being ought to have to put up with that sassy nigger she's got in the kitchen—"

"Hazel—"

"I'll be glad when they get this funeral business over with and we can leave. I don't see how come we had to come down here in the first place. The way I hear it, you and your brother weren't all that close."

"Just do what I ask, Hazel," Bud said, wearily.

"Ha. By this time I thought I would be in Florida, dancing on the patio of that big hotel where we made the reservations at. Instead here I am standing out here a hundred miles from nowhere, in this old front yard, with a body in the house been dead two years. I don't know one soul would believe this if I ever told it to them."

"Just behave yourself and see if you can't help mama out some. I got a feeling that things may work out where we could go to Florida every year if we wanted to."

"What are you talking about. You up to one of your tricks?"

"How'd you feel about moving down here to live?"

"Are you out of your mind?" She looked at him a moment, to see if he was actually serious. He seemed to be. "Move *here*? If you tell me you are serious about that, Bud Kantwith, I am going to be on the next bus heading for Tennessee. Love or money couldn't get me to live here. N. O., no. You got the wrong person for them plans, Mr. Bud Kantwith."

"I don't mean *here*. I mean in town."

"You think that is any better? What is the matter with you, anyway? What are you going to do here? Work over yonder in that picture frame factory we passed coming down here? I think you've gone crazy."

"Bevo told me something very interesting this morning."

"What could he tell you, you didn't already know?"

"Told me a lot of things."

"Well, what? I guess he told you that your daddy is worth more money than anybody else around here. Is that what he told you? I could of told you that. I could also of reminded you of the fact that we ain't never seen one penny of his money."

"About six or eight years ago, they started in drilling for oil all around here—right out there in Bogue Chitto Bottom, they must of drilled a dozen wells. I don't really remember if it was oil or natural gas they were drilling for that time, and Bevo can't remember either. But it was one or the other—"

"Bud, what in a blue moon are you talking about?"

"Getting rich. They drilled two wells right down yonder in

the pasture. Out back behind Lavina's house."

"But they didn't find nothing, did they?"

"They *said* they didn't find nothing," Bud replied.

"What is that supposed to mean?"

"Means some people around here didn't believe them. Or, more than likely, got themselves a inside source of information."

"And who would that be, if I need to ask?"

"Tom and old Joiner Whittal is who. Between them, since them folks were in here drilling them wells, they've just about bought up all the land around here—and lapping over into all the counties around here. Now how come you think they'd be doing something like that? They know something, and Bevo said that the way he hears it, Tom and Joiner made a deal with them fellows drilling them wells to back off until they'd gobbled up all the land around here. Then they're gonna call them back in, and you know who is going to be rich, don't you?"

"Either rich or crazy. I think maybe they both just may be crazy."

"Crazy like foxes. Why Bevo said daddy has got everything he owns mortgaged to the hilt from buying land—he's got more'n twice as much as old Joiner Whittal has—and some of it he paid top dollar for. Now Tom Kantwith is too smart and close with money to go around paying a nickel more than any land around here is worth, just to own it. The way Bevo figures, we are sitting right on dab top of what will become one of the richest oil fields in the country—"

"Just how do you plan to get in on it?"

"By just being Tom Kantwith's only living son is the first step. And I intend to find out how much Progress knows. I don't think Tom is pushing him off toward Camilla because he actually *likes* him."

"I don't think she can stand him. And that is one thing I'd agree with her on."

"Well, being as I am practically his brother-in-law—"

"Are you kidding? I just told you Camilla can't stand him."

"I know that and you know that. But does *he* know that? Who knows, I may offer to help him out some with Camilla—"

"Well, you better be quiet about it. Here he comes with that Bevo . . ."

"Now you mind what I told you, and see if you can't keep from fighting with Camilla just for one day."

"Hey, Bud. Old Prog here is in a mighty hurry to get back to town. You gonna drive us back over there?" Bevo Harvey asked, looking at Hazel. He nodded his head and grinned at her. Which made Hazel wonder if he had good sense and doubt the validity of what he'd told Bud about the oil wells.

"Sure thing. Now you go on in the house, out of this hot sun, hon," Bud said to Hazel.

Which she did not immediately do. She stood in the yard and watched the car as far as she could see it, and the dust it left behind, moving across the Bogue Chitto Bottom. The fact was, Hazel was intimidated by Ouida's quiet reserve and terrified of Tom Kantwith. She didn't know why, exactly. It wasn't a reasonable fear, it just was, and she avoided him as much as possible. In his presence she always felt as if she was about to make a fool of herself. She was tempted to follow Camilla around to the wisteria arbor, but she knew she'd be less welcome there than if she intruded on Tom and Ouida in the front parlor. She started, quietly, up the steps and toward the porch swing, but stopped, startled, when the three old people came out of the house. She nodded at them and quickly fled toward the store.

9

The Bogue Chitto Man

Left alone with the coffin in the front parlor when Ouida took the young soldier to the bedroom where he'd be staying, Tom Kantwith grieved, as much as he found it possible to allow himself, for his oldest son.

That their relationship had never been what it could, or should have been, was a reality that he could not ignore. That he and Perce had never been close, as close as a father and son should be, Tom had always blamed on Ouida. She had, from the very beginning, taken charge of Perce's upbringing—and his affections. Still, evèn though he'd never spoken of it to anyone, he'd always grudgingly admired the boy's independence and blatantly rebellious attitude toward parental authority, especially that of his father. By the time the boy reached puberty Tom had accepted the obvious, that they would never be friends, not in the way some men became friends with their sons. That, however, had not prevented Tom from believing that Perce would eventually take charge of his life and become a better man than his father had ever been. Tom had not only believed that would happen, he'd actually looked forward to it. But that dream had ended with a bullet in Korea.

No man could have been prouder than Tom had been the day Perce was born. December 10, 1930, and about as cold a day as he could ever remember. The kitchen pump had frozen the night before, and he'd spent most of the morning thawing out the pipe, happily laughing to himself, even proud that the baby was coming exactly to the day nine months after the wedding night. For some reason that had seemed terribly important to Tom at the time.

He'd been no more than a boy himself, having celebrated his twenty-third birthday the month before, and Ouida had turned twenty-one a couple of weeks before they were married. That morning he'd had to get Kiki—she was in the fourth grade—off to school and out of the way, as Ouida had gone into labor during the night. She'd had a difficult time, and when the baby still had not come by the middle of a cold and dreary afternoon, they'd made preparations to take her down to the hospital at Kosciusko. Then, very quickly, just as Kiki arrived home from school, the baby came. Everyone, and especially his parents, Robert and Mary Ann, had been overjoyed that it was a boy. They'd lost two sons of their own—Isaac II and Yates, born between Tom and Kiki—to diphtheria in 1921, the year before Kiki was born.

That Perce had been a true Kantwith—born with the bright blue eyes and a head covered with the dark brown curly hair peculiar to the family—had been cause for even more rejoicing. Perhaps that had been part of the trouble that came later between them; Perce had been too much Kantwith, stubborn, headstrong, and obstinate as hell when he took a notion. Kantwith men had always found it difficult to get along with one another. The feud between old Isaac and his brother, Barton, both of whom had come to Mississippi from Connecticut in the 1860s, had continued down to the present. Barton's descendants, the "other Kantwiths," lived down in Attala County and kept pretty much to themselves; not a one of them had visited Shadowland since Mary Ann's death in 1948. The only time Tom ever saw his cousin Bart was when he ran into him at a cattle auction or some such affair, or by accident on the streets of Kosciusko, which he didn't often visit. Bart had a pair of daughters that Tom wouldn't recognize if he ran into them on the street. A third one had run off to Hollywood to become a movie star after she'd won a beauty contest. Tom had been curious enough to drive all the way over to Greenwood, back before Christmas, to see her in a musical, and was somewhat proud of the fact that she hadn't made a fool of herself. He had enough fools in his own branch of the family without adding cousins he hardly knew to the list.

Ouida came into the room, walked to the coffin, and touched

the flag with her fingers. She glanced at him and walked on to the window. Camilla was sitting in the wisteria arbor. "What are you thinking? she asked, without looking at him.

"About him. About family," he answered. "Did I ever tell you that I went to Greenwood to see Bart's girl in that picture show she was in? What was her name, Willadeen?"

"Yes. She calls herself Willa Kant in the movies. They wrote her up in *Look* magazine. And in *Collier's* too. Camilla's got a copy of them in her room. What made you think of her?"

"Just things. The way things are, have turned out. You're taking it well. About Perce," he said. And, indeed, once they'd brought the coffin in the house, she'd taken hold of herself admirably, even offering the Thomsons cake and iced tea, which they'd refused. They, along with everyone else, had been eager to get on, it seemed to him.

"Where did you put that soldier?" he asked.

"In Perce's room," she replied, much to his surprise. No one had slept in the little bedroom behind the kitchen since Perce had been home last. "He'll be more private there," she added, "away from the family."

"Everybody else gone?"

"Yes. Your aunt and cousins are out on the front porch. Tom?"

"What?"

"You take it easy on Camilla. She's taking this hard. She hasn't known a death, not since your mother died. She was too little to know what it was when my folks died."

"I will. But I can't for the life of me figure out what goes on in that girl's head. She's as stubborn as—" He stopped himself before he said "Kiki." He had not once spoken her name since the night she left, carrying a bastard baby, the thought of which irritated him still, after twelve years.

"Just never mind what goes through her head, and quit pushing Progress Joiner off on her," Ouida said, turning from the window.

"I just want what's best for her."

"What you think is best may not be what's best at all. She's got her mind made up on going to college, and if that is what she wants, then that is what she will do. I'd like for one of mine to get an education, and I guess she's the only hope. Perce would of and would of made something of himself if he'd lived."

Tom could not and would not argue with that. Nevertheless, he did not like the idea of Camilla going off to college. He could never forget that his sister had, and had gotten herself mixed up with a wild crowd; had come home carrying a bastard and shaming the family before everyone. For the time being he'd let the matter of Camilla alone, but he'd not had his last say on the matter. In these times a man had to be more careful than ever where a daughter was concerned. With the exceptions of Ouida and Mavis Patton, Tom had never been able to give women credit for having much sense. Camilla had never done much to convince him that he could also make an exception in her case.

"Old Man Goodwin didn't keep his appointment with me this morning. I'm going over there to find out why."

Now Ouida turned and faced him. "Did they say where he was, at the bank?" she asked.

"No. Just that something had come up he had to take care of."

"Well why don't you just let it be, at least for today?" she asked.

"Because I can't. Something is going on, and I'm going to find out what. Three times in the last six months I've had my eye on land and somebody has grabbed it right out from under my nose . . . good land that I wanted. Goodwin knows what's going on, and he's going to tell me."

"What do you mean?" Ouida asked, remembering Old Man Goodwin's visit and wondering what Tom would do if he found out the banker had come to see her that morning. She suspected she'd find out once Kiki arrived.

"I mean that I've found out some outfit out of Texas bought those three pieces of land, and they couldn't have done that without Goodwin's help. I suspect that old Canton Chislom is behind it, is buying up land I had first dibs on in Bogue Chitto, behind my back."

"Isn't Canton Chislom the one behind that outfit that came in here that time and dug those wells looking for oil or something? I thought you said he'd died."

"He did, and that's what bothers me. When a man like that dies, banks and lawyers take over his interests, his land and oil business, and you can't trust them as far as I can throw that coffin."

"Tom! I know you didn't care all that much about him, but at least you don't have to—"

"Don't say I didn't care about my own son. I did care. I never could get to him, never could reach him, because—"

"Don't go putting blame where there is none, Tom. He was your son, but you never let him close to you. You never, ever, expected him to be a child; never complimented him once in his entire life. He's gone now, and that coffin is all we have left of him. It's too late to be putting blame. It's too late to blame yourself or anyone else for what is done."

"But Ouida, you're blaming me. You always have. You blame me for marrying you in the first place. And you blame me for fathering your children. You blame me for not being here the night little Bobby died. Would he have lived if I'd been here?"

"It wasn't me that blamed you for not being here the night the baby died, Tom. It was your own mother. Your father, too. There was nothing that could have been done to save him. I know that. And you've always blamed yourself for not being here." She turned back to the window. "And I never blamed you for *marrying* me."

"You wanted to go back to college, get your degree. That's all you used to talk about."

"If I'd wanted it bad enough, don't you think I would have done it? I can't blame you for doing something I wanted to do, marrying you. I do blame you for some of the things you've done since. Now go on about your business, if you feel that is what you have to do."

Tom walked out of the room, feeling the weight of things left unsaid. It was true, he had always felt guilty for not being home the night the baby, Robert II and named after his own father, had died; the baby that came between Bud and Camilla. He could no longer remember where he'd been that night in 1937. With a woman, he was sure of that, but he couldn't remember who she was. Had he lived, Bobby would be nineteen, and would have—Tom had long ago convinced himself—turned out somehow different from his other sons; different from Perce, certainly different from Bud.

The fact of the matter was, if there was one of his children that he actually disliked, it was Bud, who looked not one iota like a Kantwith but was the spitting image of Ouida's father, Calvin Cannon. And it was too bad he'd not also been born with that old man's good sense and gentle ways. No, as far as Tom was concerned, Bud had been born without a brain in his head and had now spent twenty-two years proving it.

If more proof was needed, the thought occurred to him as he walked out on the front porch, it was coming up the hill toward him from the store, sucking on a bottle of Grapette. How a son of his, even Bud, could actually marry and father a baby by Hazel was beyond his comprehension. Hazel was the sort of woman a man took to a bed on a Saturday night and forgot about Sunday morning; not one he married, unless he was some sort of grand champion fool. He liked her even less now that she looked as if she was going to drop twins at any moment. He had never discussed the matter of the coming blessed event with Ouida, except to acknowledge it, and had no idea that she had misgivings about becoming a grandparent. He, however, found the notion entirely repulsive. Even though his hair had turned completely white, he still had it all, and didn't feel like a grandfather in the least.

And even if he had, there was no way he could be convinced that a child by Bud out of Hazel could be less than a full-blown idiot. And she was standing there at the bottom of the steps, grinning at him like a Memphis whore, which he'd always suspected she probably had been before she latched on to Bud. A man could beget a fool—Bud was a good example of that—but in most cases it was an accident of nature. In the case standing before him, it was a foregone certainty.

"Oh, Daddy Kantwith. Bud just went running off with his friends and left me out here by myself. Ain't that just like a husband?"

The thought struck Tom's mind that it was one of the smarter things Bud had ever done in his life. "Where did he go?" he asked.

"Over to town to take Bevo and Progress back. He just loves coming down here and being with his friends, but I'm not a woman likes to be left alone."

By God, the woman was pregnant as all hell by his own son, and if she wasn't flirting with him he was a prize jackass. Tom was actually embarrassed. "Well, Hazel, how have you been? When is the baby due?"

"Not for awhile yet. None too soon to suit me, if you know what I mean!" Actually Hazel was so nervous that her legs felt weak, and she was vaguely aware that she was making a fool of herself.

As did most women, Hazel read in Tom Kantwith's casual brusqueness, his cavalier indifference and disalarming habit of giving his whole attention to the person to whom he was speaking, a sexual flattering that was not intended. Nor even thought of, at least not by Tom.

Actually, Ouida was one of the few and probably the last woman Tom had ever seduced. The rest—and there had been dozens of them since the first, a forty-three year old married woman who sexually initiated him a month after his twelfth birthday—had all seduced him. That fact had never mystified Tom the way it did most men. He simply accepted it as the way of things; women were sexual predators. They would use and allow themselves to be used by a man to get him in bed.

Tom's opinion of women was not a very catholic one; not subscribed to by any of his friends and associates. But, then, Tom Kantwith had never seen the need of discussing women with other men. It had always been a wonder to him that *they* spent so much time discussing women, as if there was some sort of great mystery about them. There was, Tom knew, no mystery.

With the exception of Ouida. Now she was, singularly, the most exceptional woman he had ever known in his life who was not his mother or one of his aunts, who, in the latter case were simply too crazy to be considered in the same light with other females of the world. Ouida had come to Bogue Chitto fresh and starchy and schoolteacherish; what Mary Ann, his own mother, referred to as "a lady." Until Ouida had come to Green Grove to teach and live at Shadowland, he had thought all women called ladies were somebody's mothers.

The first night she had stayed under the same roof with him, Tom had expected of Ouida what he had already come to expect of all women; that she would come to his bedroom in the night.

He had not, in fact, considered the possibility that she would act otherwise. When, after she'd been boarding with his parents for three weeks and still had not sought out his bed in the night, he had gone to hers and had been soundly rebuffed. That was exactly the moment he'd made up his mind that she would become his wife.

She had never willingly come to his bed and had, the last several years, barred him from her own. That did not really bother him; had in fact caused him to like her more, as most women tended to act like Alabama yard dogs in Spring heat in his presence. Tom had never given much thought to the notion that they did not all act in that manner and that those that did were not always in season to all men; it simply never occurred to him that, in this matter of female seduction, he was the exceptional quarry, available to virtually any woman—and there were many of them—who found him attractive.

That ignorance colored his opinion of women and caused him to think of them, with few exceptions, as somewhat lesser beings than men. It was not, however, an ignorance that he found uncomfortable.

To his mind the proof was in the pudding, and certainly an example of it was standing in the yard grinning at him.

"You're going to have a boy for us, aren't you?" he asked.

"I'll try. But it may just come a girl!"

"Better not. We got all the contrary females this family needs now. You just have us a big ole healthy boy, you hear?" The idea of an idiot granddaughter that looked like Hazel was a possibility that Tom was in no mood to consider.

"I'll do my very best to do just that, Daddy Kantwith! I sure will, if that'll make you happy."

"Well, now. I got to be going over to town. I got some business at the bank to get out of the way today," said Tom, expecting Hazel to get out of his way and let him be on about his business. But she was too flustered to move.

"Bud says you're buying some more land. He says you already own about all the land there is around here. That's what he said."

"Well, I suppose that is a fact," Tom replied. He couldn't bring himself to be impolite to a woman, even Hazel. On the other hand, he couldn't resist the opportunity to brag a bit for the ears of his cousins and especially Aunt Iola, spread as they were across the front porch like three turkey buzzards waiting for a carrion to get ripe enough to eat. Aunt Iola had predicted, when she'd taught him in the seventh grade, that he'd never amount to a hill of beans, and he'd never forgotten it.

"No" he said, speaking louder. "I doubt there is many men in the state of Mississippi that can lay claim to the title of more land than I can, and weren't but a paltry eight hundred acres of it left to me." He glanced around and saw that Aunt Iola was leaning forward in her chair, listening. "The day will come," he continued, "when I'll be the richest man in the state, bar none. Between me and Progress Joiner's family, we got all the good land in this part of the state sewed up, that's worth anything. Course, getting your hands on good land around here is not as easy as it used to be."

"Why is that, Daddy Kantwith?"

"Some damned bunch out of Texas—a combine—is out to beat me in getting title to what little land is for sale this past few months."

"A combine? I just don't understand all them business things," Hazel said, still flirting, in spite of better intentions.

"You can understand this one. Any idiot can. Every time I get somebody talked into selling me their land at a decent price, some outfit out of Texas has gone and bought it right out from under me. Ought to be a law against outsiders coming in here and grabbing land right out from under a taxpayer's nose."

"That is something. My!"

Tom had grown weary of the game and, besides, talking to Hazel made about as much sense as trying to carry on a conversation with a flight of bluebirds. He walked down to his car, got in and drove off. Once, before he did, he glanced back at the porch. Aunt Iola had settled back in her chair; the cousins had not changed expression or position. It seemed as if all three were waiting for something to happen. "I'll be damned," he muttered to himself, "if it don't seem they get some sort of satisfaction out of death."

Satisfaction was more than Tom found at the bank in Bolatusha. Mr. Goodwin, he was informed by Miss Black, had gone to Winona on bank business and was not expected back. That was what she had been instructed to say to anyone inquiring as to Donald Goodwin's whereabouts, and especially if that anyone was Tom Kantwith. She was as perplexed as Tom was, for she knew of no bank business that would take her employer to Winona or anyplace else, and it was not like Donald Goodwin to make up excuses to be away from the bank, especially not twice in one day. Whatever the reason, it had something to do with Tom Kantwith and the woman that had come into the bank earlier, the one that Mr. Goodwin had taken home to dinner. But Mr. Goodwin had been quite firm in instructing her not to mention Mrs. Chislom's visit to anyone. Having had access to most of the bank's records for the four years she'd been employed there, she was aware of Mrs. Chislom's interest in the bank. What she didn't know was that the woman was Tom Kantwith's sister.

Not that she would have told him in any case. Bank's business was bank's business and, besides, she intensely disliked Tom Kantwith. She was still a virgin and saw no charm in the cold blue eyes staring across the counter at her. Only after he left did it occur to her that Mrs. Chislom had those same eyes. But, then, that also was bank's business.

Matt McNeil was getting in his car when he saw Tom come out of the bank. The warrant was in the glove compartment, but he had better things to do than serve it; he had to go over to the high school and find out exactly how a person went about crowning a May Queen. He was proud that he'd been asked to do that. It was too bad Tom's daughter wouldn't be able to be there to win the damn thing. He'd always liked that feisty little ole girl.

Henry Lambert was across the street and also saw Tom come out of the bank. He stepped back in the narrow alley between two buildings to avoid being seen himself; and having to explain to Tom what he was doing in town on a Monday when there was work to be done. He still wasn't sure he believed Lavina about Tom not knowing what had happened to Jamie. On the other hand, he had not been able to find one person who'd seen his son on Saturday. Several people, colored people, had remembered seeing Jamie when he'd come to town two weeks before, but not one of them had seen him on Saturday. To his way of thinking, a grown boy didn't just up and vanish off the face of the earth—and that was exactly what he'd told Matt McNeil not thirty minutes earlier.

But the Sheriff had been no help; suggesting that maybe

Jamie had run off with some woman. As far as he knew, Jamie wasn't involved with any women.

Matt had been telling the truth when he said he hadn't heard anything about Jamie; he'd registered real surprise on his face when he'd been told that Jamie was missing. Of all the white men in Bolatusha, Matt McNeil was the one most likely to tell him the truth. And if the truth had been such that Matt couldn't, or wouldn't want to tell him, he'd have made up a lie to placate the colored community, if for no other reason. No, the Sheriff had no idea of what had happened to Jamie, of that Henry was sure. Which put him right back where he started. That meant he'd have to walk over to the west side of town, two miles, where most of Bolatusha's colored people lived, and ask more questions. He'd be lucky to get home before dark.

Had she taken her leave of the banker's wife, Gene Goodwin, five minutes earlier, Katherine Chislom would have also seen her brother come out of the bank. She drove west to Harvey's Standard and took a right on the road that would take her to Kantwith and home, not a mile behind Tom.

Tom had no desire to return home so soon, remembering the coffin and Hazel and the old people sitting on his front porch. When he came to the intersection at Salem Baptist Church, he turned right on the Vaiden road. He had not eaten anything since breakfast, and Mavis Patton's cook made the best hamburgers in the world. And besides, as he'd often said, Mavis had the coldest beer and the warmest butt in the state of Mississippi.

10

Let Me Recall His Face

"I think your daddy is the nicest man!" Hazel said, walking into the wisteria arbor and disturbing Camilla's quiet time.

"What?" Camilla asked. She had been watching Lavina walking back up toward the house.

"I said I think your daddy is the nicest man I've ever met, just about."

Camilla stared at her for a moment. "That proves right there you haven't got sense enough to think," she said.

"Well, he is just as nice as he can be to me. Just charming and all. And I think that boy, Progress? I think he's just as nice as he can be."

"You know what I think? I think you've lost your damned mind's what I think."

"Well, I know you're just all upset about Perce and all, and maybe you're not seeing things the way they really are."

"Have you been drinking shoe polish or something?"

"You know, when something gets me all upset, sometimes I don't see things the way I ought to. One time my mama got run into by some niggers in a maroon car? And they took her to the hospital? You know what I did?"

"You got a gun and shot the niggers in the maroon car?"

"No. Don't be silly. We lived way off down there by South Parkway in Memphis? And I *walked* all the way to Baptist Hospital."

Camilla stared at her, expectantly. "So?" she finally asked.

"Well, don't you see? I walked all the way to the Baptist Hospital, and I had the money for the bus or a taxi cab right in my pocket the whole time, and I never thought to get on one."

"What does that prove?"

"Well, don't you see *anything*? I had the money right in my pocket the whole time, and sometimes when I was walking all that ways I had my hand right on the money and playing with it, and I never thought to catch the bus or anything. Don't you see what that proves?"

"All it proves to me is that my opinion of you has always been just about right on the head."

"You are the meanest little bitch—"

"I think you've already told me that once today."

"Bud made me promise to be nice to you, and what do I get? A slap in the face is all. There is just no putting up with you that I can see—"

"Hazel," Ouida said, coming out the kitchen door. Would you go down to the store and ask Billy Ray to send up me a package of dry yeast?"

"There is just no getting along with her!"

"Hazel, Camilla was sitting here in the arbor minding her own business and you came out here, and the next thing I know you're yelling so's I can hear you in the house, and we've got company in there. Now there is no reason the two of you have to fuss and fight the livelong day. If you can't get along, stay away from each other, because I am sick and tired of hearing this bickering and fighting, and I am not going to put up with it any longer. Now would you please do as I've asked and go get that dry yeast from Billy Ray?"

"Well, why can't you send her after it? She's not doing one thing that I can see."

"Because I asked you to go," Ouida said, a firmness in her voice with which there would be no bargaining. She watched Hazel walk out of the arbor and around the house, her back arched stiffly, then moved over and sat down on the bench beside her daughter.

"Camilla, do you have to fight with her?"

"I don't know. I guess I do. She bugs the hell out of me."

"I've been keeping him company. Him and that soldier. It's strange . . ."

"Mama . . . ," Camilla said, and when she turned Ouida saw

the tears flowing freely down her cheeks.

"What is it?" Ouida asked and, for the first time in many years, slipped her arm around the shoulder of another—even that of her own daughter—without considering it first, without embarrassment.

"Mama . . ."

"What is it? Why don't you come in the house and talk to that young soldier? He seems like a nice young man."

"Mama, that is the whole thing. I can't."

"What do you mean, you can't?"

"I just can't . . . I . . . I just don't want to look at it right now." She turned and stared at the house: "No matter how hard I try, I just can't believe it. Bringing Perce home really is just like having him die all over again. I thought it would be better, Mama. Somehow, I thought it would make it better . . . bringing him home. But it doesn't."

"Don't sweetheart. Don't cry."

"I looked forward to this day as much as you did, Mama. To having him brought home. Mama, you know how much I loved my brother. I thought I would know it like I always knew things with Perce. When they got here with the body, I thought I would feel *different* inside . . . would feel good inside like I always did when Perce was around. I remember how he could look at me when Tom was yelling at us about something and wink and maybe smile just a little . . . You remember how he could do that?"

"I remember," Ouida said softly.

"And I would feel all warm inside without anything being spoken between us . . . Mama, I don't feel that now."

"I don't feel that either, that my Perce is near me again. That's the hard part—not knowing if it is really him they sent us in that box, or maybe just a part of him, or what. I thought I would be able to touch the coffin and know if my Perce was touching the other side of it . . . I don't want to cry anymore. But I really did think I would know if my first born had come home to me. God knows my Perce . . . God knows my baby. He brought me such happiness, your brother did. You all . . . All of you brought me love for you but it was Perce, my first born, that brought me happiness like I'd never known before. You will know that feeling, maybe, when you've had your first and marvel at yourself and at creation for having had him.

"He was such a pretty baby, with all that curly hair and those blue eyes peculiar to the Kantwiths. He and little Bobby were the only ones that took after them in looks. You and Bud took after mine . . . God! I was happy the day Perce was born. It was just so cold that I was sure he'd freeze to death on us! Oh, he was just so pretty!" Ouida stopped suddenly, realizing that she was crying and laughing at the same time. "Your father was just as proud. Just as proud as he could be. He was different then. Or maybe he wasn't . . . Maybe I just saw him in a different light then."

"Mama?"

"Now, Camilla . . . ," Ouida said, dabbing at her eyes. "What we have to do now . . . What we *both* have to do now is finally accept his death. We have to do that. Come on in the house, now."

"Maybe in a little while . . . Mama, I always remembered exactly what he looked like until they drove up here with him in that old hearse. Now I can't recall his face. I wish God would let me recall his face, because for the life of me I can't. I can't go looking at his coffin if I can't even recall his face."

Ouida stood up. "I still have to go up yonder and see about his grave. I should have gone this morning when they were up there digging it. Would you like to walk up there with me?"

"Yes," Camilla answered, then stood up and followed her mother around to the back of the house.

Lavina was sitting on the kitchen steps.

11

He Did Sing To My Jamie

"That soldier is taking a bath," she said. "I don't like to be in no house where a strange man is taking a bath."

"Well, he's not going to bite you, Lavina," Camilla said.

"Besides the point, he does or not. Them old people go on back home where they belong?"

"They were sitting on the front porch the last time I looked," Ouida replied.

"You think they're going to stay for supper?"

"I don't know. I sent Hazel to get some dry yeast from Billy Ray to make some more white bread. We'd better have plenty. Who knows how many we'll have to feed. Lavina, Camilla can help me if you want to go on back home."

"Never mind Camilla helping you. And what am I going to do at my house but sit around and mope? 'Sides, when *she* gets here you're gonna have your hands full. You thought about that?"

"I've thought about it. I guess I'll have to think more about it when it comes time to cross that bridge. We're going up to the church to see about Perce's grave."

"Go on, then. But if that old woman comes in my kitchen and starts in bossing me around like she likes to do, I'm gonna heave her right out this kitchen door. I ain't studying messing around with her today."

"Just tell her I said for her to stay out of the kitchen. She's got her own kitchen to mess up."

"When *do* you think Miss Kiki is going to show herself around here?"

"Your guess is as good as mine. Did Henry go to town?"

"He went. Henry thinks Bubba's dead."

"No. Don't think that."

"I don't know what to think anymore. My head's so full of worry I can't see straight no more. I just want to see my boy, is all. Just see him!"

"Lavina . . ."

"No, Miz Ouida. I know you'd like to see your boy, too. I know that. You don't remember that Henry and me moved in here and I started working in the house the year after Perce was born? I knew him as a baby. He was like my baby, too. I loved that boy as much as one of my own—"

"I know you did, Lavina—"

"Remember how he used to sneak off down to my house when he was little?" She looked at Camilla. "Perce was just like you was about coming to visit me when I was home. Sometimes he'd come ambling up, like he had a way of doing. Not sneaking about it, but more like some little old man on some business, and I'd say, 'Perce, what are you doing off down here?' And he'd just stand there and grin and grin. When Jamie was born, Perce come down there the very next day, saying he wanted to see the baby. Henry put that little baby in Perce's little arms, and you know what he did?"

Ouida knew; she'd heard the story dozens of times. "What did he do?" she asked.

"He started singing to that baby, 'rock a bye baby in the tree top,' and didn't know hardly any of the words to that song. Yes he did sing to my Jamie!"

"Mama?"

"Hush, Camilla."

"Yes. It was Perce, was the one that started in calling Jamie by Bubba, and that child had to be five years old before he knew for sure if his name was Jamie or Bubba. One time . . . You was too little to remember this, Camilla. But one time when Jamie was in about the second grade, Perce made him a slingshot for Christmas. Made it all by hisself and painted it red and then he taught

Jamie how to use it. I still got that slingshot. All the paint is about wore off it.

"Then the day we heard that Perce had been killed, Jamie took that slingshot out of the top drawer of his chest and brought it to me. He said, 'Here, Mama, you'll want to keep this.' "

Lavina looked off down toward her house. "I still got that slingshot right down there on my mantle board. I loved Perce, Miz Ouida. I don't want to have to grieve two boys. I sure don't want to have to do that. Now y'all go on over to the church and see about your business. You know, I had in mind to take some flowers over there for Miss Kiki's baby—" She stopped suddenly and stared at Ouida.

"Kiki's baby? What baby?" Camilla asked.

"Miz Ouida, I didn't mean to go and blurt that out. I must be crazy out of my mind to go saying something about that—"

"What baby?" Camilla asked again.

"That little grave back in the corner behind your great grandfather's is the grave of your Aunt Kiki's little baby," Ouida said flatly.

"You never told me that," Camilla protested. "You said it was my cousin's grave!"

"It is your cousin's grave."

"The one with the little white cross with nothing on it?"

"Best you tell her, she's going to find out soon enough," Lavina said. "Now that I done opened my big mouth about it."

"Tell me!" Camilla demanded.

Lavina looked at Ouida for a moment, then turned to Camilla. "That is Miss Kiki's baby," she said. "I helped to deliver that baby, and I helped to bury it. And when I think to remember, I take some flowers over there. And your mama was the one that bought and paid for that little white cross and put it there with her own hands."

"Well, why didn't somebody tell me about it? Don't you think I ought to know something like that?"

"I never told you because you never asked, and there never seemed to be the right time. Until now," Ouida said.

"When did she have a baby?"

"The night she left here," Ouida replied. "You weren't here.

It was the summer my mother took sick and I'd taken you and the boys up there to visit. When we came back home, it was all over with, and Kiki was gone. She's never been back."

"What happened? I mean, how could she have a baby and bury it in Hebron cemetery and nobody ever talks about it?"

"Oh, there has been plenty of talk about it," Lavina answered.

"I don't know what happened, exactly. Lavina knows, but she's never talked about it. It's not something a whole lot of people know about, and the little they know they've guessed at. If Lavina wants to tell you about it, she will."

"No'm, I don't guess I will."

"Well, I can't believe you all have spent day in and day out together and never talked about something like that."

"Hush, girl."

"Camilla, I've never considered it too much of my business. As far as I know, only four or five people knew *exactly* what happened and none of them have ever volunteered to tell me, and I've never asked," Ouida answered.

"But what . . . *Why*?"

"Camilla," Ouida replied, losing patience, "there are some things that are very private to those people involved, and it is up to them to talk about them if they want to. You start asking questions, and you might find out more than you want to know—"

"Lavina, please, what happened?"

Lavina stared at Ouida for a moment. "I don't *know* what happened."

"Well, you just now said that you helped deliver the baby and that you helped bury it. How could you do that if you don't know what hapened?"

Lavina stared at Ouida, a question on her face.

"Go ahead, if you feel like it," Ouida said.

Lavina took a deep breath. "There used to be some old folks, colored folks named Stovall, who worked for Mr. Old Man Goodwin—"

"Donald Goodwin?"

"No. *Old* Mr. Old Man Goodwin. Mr. Donald Goodwin was in the war at the time."

"Well?"

"It was on a Sunday night, and them ole Stovall folks, Miz Marsie and Mr. Wingate, they was on their way home from visiting their daughter, lived down toward Ethel, and driving home in their old car. They was headed back to Bolatusha where they lived, and over yonder pretty close to old Shiloh Baptist Church they come upon somebody wandering around in the middle of the road—"

"Aunt Kiki?"

"It was her, and she had on a white dress, and it was all covered with blood. They thought at first they was seeing a ghost, but they stopped never less, and Miss Kiki, she come over to the window of the car and begged them to help her. Except they had one of them little ole two seat cars like they used to make back before that war, and they couldn't get her in the car."

"What happened? What did they do?"

"If you'll hush for a minute, I'll tell you. Miss Kiki told Old Wingate Stovall to come fetch me, and his wife stayed there by the road with Miss Kiki. I was in bed when Old Wingate Stovall come banging on my door and told me where Miss Kiki was, and that it looked like she was having a baby. I got in the car with him, and we went back over there . . ."

A look of pain crossed Lavina's face, and, for a moment, she was lost in thought. "We got there, and sure enough Miss Kiki was having a baby. Right there in the grass beside the road."

"Good Lord! Where was daddy . . . Tom?"

"I don't know where he was, and I didn't care where he was on account of I was studying Miss Kiki, 'cause I thought she was dying. She was bleeding bad, and that baby was already dead when she had it. It wasn't a full term baby. Me and that Old Mrs. Stovall stayed with her, while Mr. Wingate drove to town and brought back Mr. Old Man Goodwin and some blankets for her. We got her in his car, and he went and found a doctor for her. That was the last time I ever saw Miss Kiki. The next day, that Mr. Thomson was here this morning brought out that little baby in a little white casket, and we buried it. Him and me and a preacher he got from somewhere."

"But where was Tom? Didn't he even go to the funeral?"

"Camilla, she told you that he wasn't here."

"No she didn't. Was he here?"

Lavina took a moment to answer. "He wasn't here the next day. I didn't see him."

"But . . . ?"

"No more buts about it. I told you what I know about it, and that is all I know. Next time I saw Mr. Old Man Goodwin, he told me that Miss Kiki was gone and he didn't expect she would be coming back. And he was right about that. I never said nothing else about it, and them old Stovall people didn't either. Back then colored folks knew better than going around talking about something like that about a white lady."

"But where did she go?"

"You'll have to ask her that. I ain't heard word one from her since I helped put her in that banker's car that night, and her about half dead"

"Mama?"

"Camilla, you know as much about it as I do. Which is more than I knew when I woke up this morning."

"But what was she doing out there at night by herself in the middle of nowhere?"

Ouida and Lavina stared at each other for a long moment. Lavina shook her head.

"Well, you must have some *idea* why—"

"Some idea ain't the why of anything," Lavina answered. "Now you asked me, and I told you, and if there is any more to it you want to know, you'll have to ask somebody who knows," Lavina sobbed. None of them were aware of exactly when she started crying.

"Camilla, are you coming over to the church with me?"

"Yes'm."

"Y'all take your time," Lavina said, as they started off, taking the path through the woods to the church.

Hazel stood at the corner of the house, next to the pump shed, with the package of yeast clutched in her sweating palm. Bud had once told her that his Aunt Kiki had a baby that died. And was born out of wedlock. She wondered if even he knew where and how it died, or that it was buried over at the church with the rest of the family. Quietly, she turned and walked back to the front of the house.

Lavina sat on the kitchen steps, rocking back and forth, and watched Ouida and Camilla take the path into the woods, singing softly:

I hear a mighty voice a'calling
I hear footsteps in the sky
I see a bright light a'shining
I see a bad time a'coming
The Lord is on his way
Sinners will have to stay
The Lord is on his way
He'll be coming here today!
I see the sea a'parting, I see
Heaven's light flashing. I see
The fire in the morning, I hear
A crying in the land!
The Lord is on his way
Sinners will have to stay
The Lord is on his way
He'll be coming here today!

12

Did He Dance On My Baby's Grave?

The glare of the afternoon sun off the white porch wall had driven the old people into the house, where they'd taken refuge in the cool front parlor. There they fanned themselves around Perce's coffin, but with their backs turned toward the bier, all seemingly staring at the same spot on the door, like some ancient protective band of Druid priests guarding the journey of the dead.

Hazel, after delivering the yeast to Lavina, went into the parlor for a better look at the coffin, but quickly fled from the grim and penetrating collective stare. She retreated to the front porch, cursing Bud, the entire Kantwith family, Mississippi, and everything in it.

She walked down the steps and was on her way back to the store to get another Grapette from Billy Ray, when she saw the dust from a fast moving automobile coming across Bogue Chitto Bottom. She paused, hoping it might be Bud returning, and cursed again when the car reached the store and slowed down. At first it looked as if the driver was going to continue on up Old Indian Ridge toward the church, but it came on instead, directly toward Hazel and the house. It was a Cadillac bearing Texas license plates. Hazel had not heard enough of the conversation at the back of the house to fathom that Katherine Kantwith was coming home and, therefore, had no idea who the woman might be, getting out of the car.

"Hello," Katherine smiled. "Are you the girl? Camilla?" Getting no reply, she walked around Hazel and started up the steps. Still smiling, she turned and asked: "Honey, are you married? Or just in trouble?"

"I'm married," Hazel replied. "And I ain't in no trouble. And I ain't Camilla, either," she added, turned, and quickly walked off toward the store.

"Well, pardon me all to hell," Kiki said and opened the door. "Hello. Is there anyone in there? Someone come to the door. You have company."

Immediately a soldier came bounding down the hall stairs, smiling. "Sorry," he said. "I was upstairs watching television. You know they get amazingly good reception way out here?"

"No, I didn't know that. The last time I was here, they didn't have television. The whole world didn't have television. Who are you?"

"Corporal James Lyon Hansen," the soldier replied.

"I see. But who in the hell are you? The Kantwith family still lives here, don't they? I just now ran into the strangest pregnant woman, who, I found out, is not my niece, Camilla, for which I suspect I am going to be very grateful, but I didn't find out who in the hell she *is*. And I don't know who you are. Who *are* you?"

"I came with the body, ma'm."

"I see."

"James Lyon Hansen, ma'm," he said, extending his hand.

"Corporal Hansen . . . Glad to meet you. Little Perce, the oldest boy. He was killed in Korea, right?"

"That is correct, ma'm."

"You came with the body?"

"That is correct, ma'm."

"Why?"

"Why what, ma'm?"

"Why did you come with the body?"

"I was ordered to. I'm the burial detail."

"The burial detail. I thought they sent two of you? Don't they usually send two?"

"They were short of men. And my C.O. said this one would be easy."

"Your C.O. owes you one. Is any of the family around, or just that strange pregnant woman?"

"The mother . . . Mrs. Kantwith, she said she was going over to the church, but I don't really know where that is, and I think the girl, Camilla, went with her. There's some relatives in the front room with the deceased. And Lavina is in the kitchen."

"Lavina?"

"Yes ma'm. She's the housekeeper."

"I know who she is," Kiki replied and started down the hallway. Then she stopped and looked back. "Who was that? The pregnant woman?"

"That was the other Mrs. Kantwith. The brother's wife."

"I see. Thank you, James." She opened the parlor door and walked in to face her aunt and cousins fanned around the casket, staring at her. The scene reminded her of a story an Egyptologist from Tulane University had told her, about how the bodyguards of Pharoahs were sealed into the tombs to guard their masters in the afterlife and sat about the bier wearing fierce expressions until all the oxygen was gone and they died. These three, however, looked rather hale, and nowhere near death. They'd all leaned forward in their chairs when she entered the room. The old woman spoke first: "Would you step forward a bit, please? Out of the shadow?"

Kiki stepped forward. "How are you, Aunt Iola? And it is cousins Weir and West, isn't it?"

"Well, Katherine. Where did you come from? I haven't seen you in some years, it seems."

"It has been some years, Aunt Iola."

"Did you ever get your degree from the university?"

"No. No, I didn't."

"Never thought for one minute you would. Never did think you and that brother of yours would amount to a hill of beans. Of course he *thinks* he's the greatest thing since sliced bread. Said it a million times. Said those two children of Mary Ann's will never amount to a thing. Of course our brother was just as much at fault as she was in spoiling the two of you rotten. That was the trouble, right there. Now if they'd sent you on down to Milsaps like I advised them to do, maybe somebody down there would have knocked some sense into your head and you'd had a starting chance in life. Or even up to Blue Mountain where Ouida went, although I never have figured out how anyone could learn much at a Baptist college. But they'd of taken the starch out of you. So what do you do? Wait tables?"

"To tell you the truth, I have waited tables," Kiki replied.

"See!" the old woman said and leaned back in her chair, an expression of smug satisfaction on her face.

Kiki glanced at the coffin and retreated from the room.

"Lavina?" she called as she opened the door to the kitchen.

"Oh, my Lord! Is that you, Miss Kiki?" Lavina said, wiping the flour off her hands. "Is it really you? My Lord in Heaven! Is it really you, come home at last?"

"In the flesh. What there is left of it," she answered, meeting Lavina's embrace and kissing her on the cheek. "Lord, I've missed you. I've missed everything about you."

"Is that a fact now, Miss Prissy," Lavina replied, holding her at arm's distance. "How come you ain't let me hear from you in all these years? Now you just do some explaining about how come you never let me hear one word from you in all these years. I can *read*, you know."

"And so can my brother. As I recall the mail comes through his little store—"

"Lord, we ain't had the post office at the store for I don't know how many years now. The mail comes by delivery from Bolatusha now. Let me take another look at you. How come you so skinny?"

"Probably because there is not one soul in all of Houston, Texas, that can cook half as well as you can."

"Houston, Texas? Is that where you're coming from?"

"That's where. How have you been, Lavina?"

"Bout the same is how. How else is there to be around here?"

"I just saw Aunt Iola. She's still the same . . . And a pregnant woman—"

"That's Bud's wife, Hazel. Pardon me, *Miss* Hazel."

"I thought she'd be a Miss Hazel. Unfriendly cuss, isn't she?"

"You don't know the half of it. Her and Camilla been going at it this whole day."

"Camilla. How is she?"

"About the same you was when you were her age. Feisty as they come, and full of vinegar and spit, and don't get along with that brother of yours any better than you ever did. You gonna like her."

"I'm anxious to see her . . . and Ouida. The soldier said they'd gone over to the church?"

"Not twenty minutes ago."

"Where is Tom?"

"Your guess is as good as mine where that one has got off to."

"Perhaps I'd better drive over to the cemetery. I've never seen my baby's grave."

"No, you ain't. We took care of it, Miz Ouida and me."

"Yes, I know. I just found that out today, and I thank you. I really mean that . . . Oh, Lavina, it is good to see you."

"You don't stop, you gonna make me start in bawling on you. Last time I saw you, I just about gave you up for dead. Old Man Goodwin told me you'd pulled through. He told me that later."

"With a great deal of help from him. Did he tell you that, too?"

"No, but I figured that much out for myself . . . You go on over yonder and see Miz Ouida. Best you say your hello to her before your brother comes busting in here, 'cause he don't know you're coming . . . Miz Ouida, she put up a little cross on the baby's grave."

"Yes, I know. And my brother? What did he do? Did he dance on my baby's grave?" There was a sharp, bitter edge to her voice that surprised Lavina.

"No, Miss Kiki. He ain't never said one word about you, not since you left here. Not a word! And I been telling Miz Ouida for all these years that ain't no natural way for a man to act—"

"Lavina, we'll talk later. I think I'd better get over there and talk to Ouida."

"You do that. You go on and do that. On this day, that woman needs somebody to talk to besides me."

"Oh? What do you mean?"

"I mean she is taking this hard. Camilla, too. They both thought the sun rose and set on Perce."

"I see. And Tom? How did he feel about Perce?"

"Whoowee! You think you and him didn't get along? Y'all got along like a preacher and chicken compared to him and Perce!"

"I see," Kiki said, thoughtfully. "We'll have time to talk later. I'd better go see Ouida before it's too late . . ."

"Too late?" Lavina asked. "Too late for what?"

But Kiki was already out the door.

13

Where The Tall Oaks Grow

The weathered clapboard church was very much as Kiki remembered it; sitting very close to the road and in a grove of white oaks near the crest of Old Indian Ridge, with a spire that had, for many years, been the tallest in all of Bogue Chitto. Farther up, at the top of the hill, the road split, with the right branch leading up to Iola's house and the left a continuation of the gravel highway that ran from Bolatusha to Wardsville.

Kiki pulled up beside the church that sat at an angle to the road and stopped. It was an isolated place, lonely, and Kiki remembered that as a child she'd found the place frightening. The cemetery, huge for a country church, covered the entire hillside on both sides of the road. The first Kantwith plot was in a grove of cedars down behind the church, near the spring and the path that ran to Shadowland; there was a newer plot just across the road from the church. The freshly dug grave—Perce's resting place—was there like a red scar on the earth, but no one seemed to be around.

Kiki wondered if the people from Kosciusko had delivered the stone for her baby's grave yet. Since learning that Ouida had long ago marked the baby's resting place, she was beginning to have second thoughts. In any case, it was probably too late to do anything about that, even if she wanted to.

"Damn," she said, as she got out of the car and slammed the door, sure that Ouida and Camilla had already left, taking the old path back through the woods. Then the side door of the church was opened, and Ouida came out.

"Ouida?"

"Lord," Ouida said, coming forward with her hands extended. "I wouldn't have recognized you in a million years."

"Have I really changed that much?" Kiki asked, taking Ouida's hands in her own for just a moment, then, on impulse, hugging her.

Ouida responded to the hug for just a moment, then pulled back, embarrassed. "No, I really wouldn't have recognized you. You're so thin! And your hair is different. You look like a different person."

"Is that bad? Do I look that bad?"

"I didn't say bad. Just different. You were a girl when I last saw you . . . But you're a woman now. I always wondered what sort of woman . . . What you'd look like when you . . . I don't know what I'm saying. You were such a pretty girl—"

"Oh? And I'm not pretty anymore?" Kiki laughed.

"Of course you are. You look like some picture off the cover of a magazine, but different. And your hair!"

"It's called frosting, and it seems to be all the rage these days, at least where I come from. There's a young man in Houston that can get miracles out of a bottle—"

"Houston? Is that where you live?"

"Yes. Didn't Donald Goodwin tell you?"

"No, he didn't. He warned me that you were coming, but he didn't say from where . . . Oh, was I supposed to tell you that he'd warned me you were coming here?"

"He told me. Ouida, about your son—"

"It's not easy,," she said, looking across at the grave. "But I'm getting used to it. What else could I do?"

"I'm sorry, Ouida. I remember him as a beautiful little boy, of course. It was so long ago. I'm truly sorry."

"Yes, we . . . But you. Somehow I didn't think you would ever come back. And now you have. And so changed!"

"I guess we all have. You've changed, Ouida. I can see that."

"Time hasn't stood still for any of us. But you! You turned into a fine looking woman, if you don't mind my saying so."

"I don't mind. At my age every compliment helps."

"Posh. How old are you? Thirty-five?"

"Pretty close."

Ouida turned suddenly and looked at the other woman carefully. "Katherine, why . . . ? I mean after all these years, why—"

"Why have I come back?"

"Yes."

"I'm sorry to arrive at a time like this. With the boy's funeral on your hands. But I had no way of knowing." She dug in her purse for a cigarette, then lit it. Still staring at Ouida, she said quietly. "That's not true. I knew."

"You knew? You knew about Perce? That they were bringing him home today?"

"Yes. I knew."

"You came for the funeral, then?"

"Not exactly. I don't really know why I came back here. I had some business with Donald Goodwin. My husband died a few weeks ago—it was after a long illness—and I suppose it just seemed like a good time to come. He—my husband—never wanted me to come back . . .

"To tell you the truth, Ouida, I've planned it for years, coming back. You surely must have known that one day I would. But I really can't tell you exactly why." She turned and walked, paced, toward the grave across the road. "My business with Donald was important, but not so important . . . Somewhere in the back of my mind there is a reason, but, out of choice, I suppose, I haven't really thought much about it. That's not true, either. Ouida, you're making this very hard for me."

"If not for the funeral, then why come back now? At this time that is so hard for us? Why couldn't you wait, at least until it was over? How did you know about it. About Perce and the funeral?"

Katherine stopped and looked down at the grave that was covered with planks. "Ouida, I really did come back for the funeral. But not with the best of intentions. It was what I wanted all along. To see you—no, not you! To see Tom. To see Tom Kantwith at the burying of one of his own—"

"Katherine . . . "

"No, wait. But you weren't here, were you? You were visiting your folks when I came home and Tom threw me out. You weren't here . . . "

"No," Ouida said softly.

"Ouida, where is my baby's grave?"

"Down behind the church. In the old plot. He's next to your grandfather. I don't know why they put him there. I . . . Mama died, and when I came back . . . Camilla is down there—"

"I'm anxious to see her," Katherine said and started walking away.

"Katherine, wait."

"Yes?"

"Camilla. She didn't know about your baby until today. Not until a little while ago. Lavina told her just before we came over here."

"The deep, dark family secret?"

"No. It wasn't like that."

"How was it, then?"

"Hardly anyone knew. . . knows. God only knows how. . . But Old Man Goodwin must have taken care of any gossip there was. To tell you the truth, I didn't know myself what happened that night, until Lavina told me and Camilla just a while ago. I didn't know until then where you'd had the baby, or any . . . No one would ever talk about it, not even Lavina."

"Tom never told you?"

"Tom never mentioned one word about it. Not a word in all these years."

"He never talked about what happened that night? Between us?"

"No. I've always suspected something happened, but I never knew what. Did he know you were . . . were going to have a baby?"

"My God. Of course he knew. I didn't come home that summer because I was pregnant. Finally my friends ran out of hospitality and I ran out of money, and I had to come back. I came back to ask Tom's help. He didn't give it to me. He kicked me out of my own house, a house that was as much mine as it was his. I had my baby beside the road. And when I was having my only child—the only child I will ever have—I still wore the imprint of my brother's hand on my face and the bruises on my body from his pushing me out of the house and down the steps." She turned and stared at Ouida, full face. "It was murder, Ouida. Your husband murdered my baby—all my babies, for after that I could never have another . . ."

"Katherine . . . Kiki . . ." Ouida reached out, and the woman came into her arms. "I didn't know . . . I didn't know. I never even guessed."

Katherine pulled away, found a scarf in her purse, and wiped her face with it. "No one knew. Just Old Man Goodwin. He knew. And my husband. Now I will see Tom bury one of his own," she added, her voice turning hard, cruel. "Now you see?"

"See what, Katherine?"

"Why I chose this time to come back here. Revenge, Ouida, for revenge. To be able to look in your faces when you buried your child, to see your tears and hear your cries."

"You can look at my tears now, Katherine."

"I know. I knew when Donald Goodwin told me about the marker you put on the grave that I'd made a mistake. It won't fill my life with joy to see your tears, Ouida. I know that your tears have been many. And I know now that there will be no tears from Tom. I should have known that he wouldn't care much more for your children than he did for mine."

"Don't say that. He cares . . . "

"Does he, Ouida? Has he changed, my brother?"

"It's been so long. Twelve years. That's a long time, Katherine."

"Is it, Ouida?"

"Tom has changed. And you. You've changed so much I hard . . . I hardly know you."

"You really didn't expect me to stay the same silly little girl forever, did you? I suppose Tom did. But being a woman, I thought you would know better."

"What is it?" Ouida asked suddenly. "What is it you want, Katherine? You're . . . yes, you're right. I doubt that you'll see him cry, even at Perce's burying in that grave there."

"I don't know what I want. I don't know what I want here. What I want I didn't have to come here for. I can make Tom Kantwith cry without coming near him. But a long time ago, that night he threw me out . . . That night I came back here for help, because I had no place else to go, no one else to turn to, and he threw me out, I swore that the day would come when I would return and I would be stronger than Tom Kantwith. And I swore . . . sitting beside the . . . my baby in my arms . . . I swore I would make him suffer dearly. All this time, I have waited until I could make him grovel to me. And he will, Ouida. He will."

"Katherine?"

"No. Wait. I am stronger than he is, Ouida. The only thing Tom understands is money and power. I have more money than he's ever seen, and power? I *own* the people he's been running around doing business with. I guess that is what I want here, Ouida. I want to see how well Tom Kantwith suffers. There. That's my reason. I want to see it with my own eyes."

"What do you mean, you own the people he's been doing business with?"

Katherine laughed, but there was no mirth in it. "This very day, Tom is running about like a chicken with its head cut off trying to buy the old Crenshaw place."

"How . . . How do you know that?" Ouida asked, not yet connecting Donald Goodwin.

"That's what he's been doing for about six years now—running about and sweating, and going out of his mind borrowing the last dime he can get his hands on to buy land, slobbering over all the land he owns. Or thinks he owns. Do you know how much land brother Tom owns, Ouida?"

"I don't know . . . He's land poor, that I know."

"Truer words were never spoken."

"What have you got to do with all this? You tell me, Katherine. For years now, Tom Kantwith has been acting like he has gone crazy. All he has done is borrow money and buy land, as if there were gold mines around here. People in Bogue Chitto are beginning to think he's taken leave of his senses—"

"And he hasn't told a soul why he was doing that, not even you. I didn't think he would."

"Katherine, you don't have to tell me what this is all about, but I wish you would. I really do," Ouida pleaded, softly.

"Tom Kantwith is under the impression that all of Bogue Chitto is floating on a sea of oil. That's the reason he's been buying every scrap of it in sight for all these years."

"There is no oil, is there?"

"Not one bucketful. Oh, there is a little bit, but it would cost you a hundred times what it's worth to get it out of the ground," Katherine replied.

"And somehow you tricked him?"

"Not somehow, Ouida. Remember when they drilled for oil a few years ago, down in Bogue Chitto Bottom? And even came over and drilled a well down near Lavina's house?"

"They didn't find a thing but rocks and water."

"They didn't even find that down by Lavina's, because they only drilled about ten feet. My late husband was in the oil business. We were drilling over across the river, and I hired those men to come here and pretend they were drilling. And Tom Kantwith jumped to the bait like a hound dog after a rabbit. Just like I knew he would, he sat down there and watched those men from sunup to sundown for three solid weeks, with the juices running out of his mouth. And then, when they pretended they could bring up oil, do you know how much Tom paid them not to? He paid those men two thousand dollars each to go back across the river and say there was no oil here—just as I knew he would do. And that was when he started buying up land like a madman. Of course he had to go to the bank, and Old Man Goodwin didn't let him make too big of a fool of himself. Not with *my* money."

"Old Man Goodwin . . . Donald's father. He helped you trick Tom?"

"Yes. He came and got me, out by Shiloh Church that night. He hated Tom almost as much as I did. Or perhaps still do."

"I still don't understand. If there's no oil, then . . . I just don't understand. Donald Goodwin said, he said something about factoring Tom's loans and things. You're the factor?"

"Yes. I also own a majority of the stock in Donald's bank. Technically, he's employed by me. And when I call in the cards, there will be no land. Revenge is a very powerful emotion, Ouida. A long time ago I set out to destroy Tom, to let him think he would get everything in the world he thought he wanted. With the plan of eventually taking it all back. All of it."

"Even the house."

"No. I have no use for the house. *You* can have the house. You can let Tom stay on or send him packing off to Mavis Patton. That's up to you."

It was several moments before Ouida replied. She turned and looked back at Perce's grave. "There was a time when I might have done that, but I still don't understand, if there is no oil.

What do *you* want with all that worthless land Tom's been buying?"

"I didn't say the land is entirely worthless. Old Man Goodwin—and Donald after him—kept him from buying entirely worthless land, like the Crenshaw place. They only let him buy the parcels that might be worth something one day, and buy it with my money—money from the little sister he called a no good worthless whore. And now I am going to collect my debts from Tom, Ouida. All of them."

"For the life of me, I can't see people, a brother and sister, carrying on like this. I don't see any sense in it at all."

"You wouldn't, Ouida. You're not the kind to understand it. But Tom is."

"I didn't tell him you were coming."

"Were you afraid to?"

"I dont know. There was never the right moment. He only came home for a little while when they brought the body, and then he left again. Then he went off looking for Old Man . . . for Donald Goodwin again. What will happen when he finds him?"

"Donald will tell him the facts of life."

"There's no telling what he's liable to do."

"No, there isn't. But I'm not afraid of what he might do. You shouldn't be either."

"No. I haven't been *afraid* of Tom for a very long time now . . ."

A warm wind stirred the upper branches of the huge old oaks, as Katherine followed Ouida around the church and down the path that led to the old Kantwith plot at the rear of the graveyard, and beyond, through the woods to Shadowland. There, at the bottom of the hill, near where the first Hebron Church had stood, Ouida continued on through the woods.

For several minutes Katherine stood and watched Camilla. She'd gathered wildflowers from the woods and put them in an old jar next to the little white cross. Now, with her bare hands, she was cleaning the weeds from the grave.

14

Allies Among The Dead

Camilla was angry and hurt that no one, not Ouida, not even Lavina, had ever told her about the baby. It didn't seem fair that, in all these years, all the time she had come to the church, she had never known about Kiki's baby. She was also angry at herself for never being curious enough to inquire, to question anyone about the grave there in the old corner of the cemetery, marked by the little white cross. It made her feel somehow betrayed.

It was several minutes before she became aware that she was not alone, that someone else was in the cemetery and watching her. For a moment she was frightened.

"Mama?" she said, then turned and saw the woman standing not thirty feet behind her, next to the cedar trees. Slowly she got to her feet, wiping the soil from her hands onto her shirt. She became aware of the sounds, of the insects in the grass, the bluejays quarreling up the oak trees, and, far off, the caw of a crow, as the woman began walking toward her, smiling. She was, in fact, the most elegant, the most beautiful woman Camilla had ever seen, far more beautiful than was indicated by any of the old photographs they had stored away at the house.

"You're my Aunt Kiki."

"Camilla," the woman said and held out her arms.

"You'll get your clothes dirty. I'm filthy."

"I have other clothes, only one niece!"

The woman wrapped Camilla in her arms. She smelled as expensive as she looked.

"My God! It's uncanny," Katherine said, holding Camilla at

arm's length. "I think I looked just like you at your age."

"Mama said just this morning that I didn't take after the Kantwiths at all in looks. I've been cleaning off the grave . . ."

"I see you have. I've never seen it before."

"You want me to leave?"

"No. No, of course not. I've long since gotten over . . . I'm glad they put him down here. It's quiet here, peaceful."

The woman stared at the grave for a long time. Camilla stepped back and watched, half expecting her to cry. On the contrary, she showed no emotion at all.

"I've . . . I learned to accept it a long time ago. But I always dreaded coming here, seeing his grave. I could have come before, many times. I've visited friends in Greenwood several times. Once my husband and I stayed there for a month. We even drove over this way, but I couldn't bring myself to come here then. I wasn't ready."

She looked off up the slope, past the old moss covered stones. "Now that I have come, it's not nearly as bad as I always thought it would be." She turned to Camilla and smiled. "Thank you for this, for the flowers."

"I just found out today—"

"I know. I saw your mother up at the church. She's gone back to the house. She said you could ride back with me," Kiki said and sat down beside the grave of her son. "Sit down and tell me about yourself. Let's talk."

"I always wanted to know you!" Camilla said, taking a seat in the grass nearby.

"And I you. It's strange, having a niece. Especially one that looks exactly like I did at your age."

"Ha. I think you just don't remember what you looked like. We have some pictures of you."

"Now I really don't know what to say to you. How is everyone . . . How are they taking Perce's . . . ?" Oddly, Katherine Chislom really didn't know what to say.

"Mama is taking it hard. And Lavina. I guess I am, too. He was my favorite."

"And your father? Tom?"

"More than likely he's too busy riding herd on the hired help, and everyone else that'll let him, to even notice," Camilla said with a trace of bitterness that did not go unnoticed by Kiki.

"So he's still riding herd, is he? Does he ride herd on you?"

Camilla laughed. "He tries. He does as much as I'll let him. From what I've heard, I guess I'm a little bit like you. Perce, he remembered you. He used to tell me about you some, when we were little. He didn't put up with Tom either. I heard you didn't take a lot of crap off him."

"No. No, I guess I didn't. Now tell me about you. Now that I've found my niece I want to know everything. You know, so many times, all these years, I've wondered about you. What you looked like. I've forgotten how old you are. How old are you?"

"Seventeen, come December first."

"That would make you what in school?"

"I'm a senior. I skipped a grade."

"You must be a lot smarter than I was. And you really are lovely. I'll bet you're the most popular girl in school."

"Are you kidding?"

"No. I'm not. Now tell me about yourself. Tell me about school."

"Well, I'm in this contest to be May Queen—"

"Really! I bet you win."

"The contest is tonight. I can't go."

"Oh, because of the . . ."

"Yes. But I don't guess it makes much difference. I wouldn't win anyway."

"Did you really want to win? Oh, of course you did."

"Sure. It's just a crappy old high school contest, but I guess I really wanted to win. It would have been nice, just once, to have been something. Do you know what I mean? I mean, I've been going to that old school all my life, and I have never been elected one solitary thing, except for class vice president about three times . . . Yes, I guess I really did want to win. To be something. You know, instead of just plain old Camilla Jean Kantwith, who gets good grades and is liked by boys and girls alike. When you were going to school there, you were elected to *everything*! You were May Queen and Homecoming Queen and Miss BHS and everything!"

"How do you know that?"

"They got all the old yearbooks in the library."

"They would. Well, I don't really remember being May Queen, but I certainly remember being Homecoming Queen. It was an experience one couldn't easily forget."

"What happened?"

"Well," Kiki laughed, remembering. "We had this crazy old home ec teacher, Miss Jewel Bell Ball—"

"She's still there. Still crazy, too—"

"Well, Miss Jewel Bell was in charge of the homecoming festivities, and she got this nutty idea of having the queen—myself—and her court wear capes over our gowns. I think crepe paper must have been a big thing in those days, because she had her home ec students make us these damned capes out of all different colored crepe paper. Mine was purple, of course, since I was the queen. Oh, God, the others were all different colors, green, yellow, red. I think poor old Maidy Ruth Woods even had a turquoise one. I remember we played Ackerman for homecoming—"

"We played them homecoming this year too. They beat us about forty to nothing."

"I don't remember how the football game came out, but what happened was, at halftime . . . Well, it had been threatening to rain all day, and at halftime, there we were, all out there on this platform they'd put up in the middle of the football field being crowned, when suddenly there came a flash of lightning and a roll of thunder, and all hell broke loose. Rain started coming down in sheets! Well, you can imagine what that rain did to the dye in that crepe paper. Not only did it dye our gowns, it dyed us too. We looked like a bunch of Easter eggs!"

Camilla laughed. "You mean it dyed your *skin*?"

"Skin, hair, and everything else. You know Miss Jewel Bell. Those capes were as big as tents and had collars that came up around our heads. Of course, when the downpour started, we were dumb enough to pull the crazy things up over our heads. I'll bet I was the only Homecoming Queen that school ever had with purple hair!"

They were silent for a moment, both of them looking at the wildflowers Camilla had gathered for the grave.

"You don't think there's a chance your mother will let you go to the dance tonight?"

"No. Anyway, I don't have anything to wear, or anyone to go with, least not anyone I'd want to go with."

"That's easily fixed. You and I are about the same size, except for height. I don't have any boobs either. And I saw a very handsome young soldier down at the house who seemed very nice. He even has manners."

"No, she'd never let me. And I don't know if I'd feel right . . . Anyway, you haven't told me anything about yourself. I don't even know where you live. You said you have a husband?"

"Had. I was married twice—"

"Where did you go when you left here? I mean, I don't know anything at all about you."

"What do you want to know?"

"Everything!"

"Everything?"

"Until today I didn't even know about the baby. Lavina, she slipped and let that out and told us about some of what happened that night. To tell you the truth, I was mad that no one had ever told me. But I guess Lavina was the only person that knew anything. Mama didn't even know, you know, about what happened, and those old Stovall negroes that worked for Old Man Goodwin . . . Where do you live?"

"Texas. Houston."

"Boy, I envy you."

"*You* envy me?"

"Sure. You got away from here, from Bogue Chitto. Did you know Willadeen Kantwith? She's our cousin? She went to Hollywood and became a movie star."

"I know. Willa Kant. She was in Houston not long ago. They had a reception for her at the Shamrock Hotel. She kept staring at me."

"You didn't tell her who you were?"

"No. I wasn't ready to open that can of worms yet. Don't tell me that's what you want to do, become a movie star?"

"Lord no. I was too shy to ever even try out for cheerleader. I haven't thought too much about what I want to be. But one thing I know, as soon as I graduate, and that's in two weeks, I plan to get away from here," Camilla said emphatically.

"What are you going to do? What do you plan to be?"

"Going to college, if Tom will let me. He's not too high on my going, and, besides, he seems to sort of have other plans for me—"

"The Whittal boy?"

"How do you know about that?"

"Donald Goodwin told me. That's dumb and stupid and typical of Tom. He once tried to marry me off to that boy's *father*!"

"Well, I don't really know what I'm going to do, but marrying Progress Whittal is not on my list of things to do. Actually, I don't really know. And it doesn't make much difference what I do, just as long as it is someplace other than here. Sometimes . . . Sometimes I think it would be nice to be married someday. To be married to a handsome man who loved me, and live in a city—in a house on a corner, with a big green yard. That's all. Other times I think, you know, I'd like to be all sorts of things."

"Regardless, you have years to think about those things. I think you should go to college, if that's what you want."

"Tom has a fit every time I mention it."

"Leave your father to me. I'll give him so many fits, what you do will be the last of his worries. And if he won't pay for it, or can't, I have money." She reached over and hugged Camilla. "Don't worry your pretty head about that sort of thing anymore. What about your brother, Bud? What's he like? I met his wife briefly. Very briefly."

"She's a bitch. And Bud is a bit like Tom, in some ways. That is, he would be like him if he had the guts. On Bud, it just comes off sneaky."

Kiki laughed. "You sure do have a way of speaking your mind, don't you?"

"Around here that's about all you can do. I guess that's the only way I've gotten by this long with Tom. By letting him know I'm not taking a whole lot of crap off him."

"I'm glad it worked out with you. With me it wasn't that easy."

"You and him didn't get along, did you?"

"Not getting along is not the word for it. No," she added, "Brother Tom and I most definitely did not get along. He was quite a bit older, fourteen when I was born, and he always acted as if he owned me. My parents—you remember mama?"

"Yes. She died when I was about ten."

"She went blind when I was a little girl, and daddy died when *I* was about ten. After that, Tom just took charge, and there wasn't much I could do about it. All the time I was growing up, he chose my friends, told me where I could go and couldn't go. He was a damned monster."

"He hasn't changed very much, and pretty much has treated me the same way. Although Mama does stand up to him a little more than she used to, since Perce got killed. He won't talk about you. Mama told us never to mention you around him."

"That figures. And your mother? Did she ever talk about me?"

"Sometimes. Lavina more. They talk about you sometimes."

"Did she ever tell you why you weren't supposed to mention my name around Tom?"

"No. But I heard it was because you had a fight and left home—a falling out. Then when Lavina told me about the baby . . . Well, I didn't know about that before, but now I suspect there was more to it than that. There was, wasn't there?"

"Yes."

"Bud always hinted that he knew something about you that I didn't. Why did you leave? It had something to do with the baby, didn't it?" Camilla asked, and looked at the grave.

"Yes. I was going to have a baby. This baby . . ."

"And you weren't married?"

"No. No, I wasn't married."

"I guess Tom threw you out for that?"

"You might say that."

"Boy, that must of took some nerve. Considering the fact that Tom Kantwith probably wasn't any closer to being a preacher then than he is right now."

"Well, he did. But I don't think it was a question of morals. Tom never had any morals of his own. Just ones he borrowed from others, when it suited his purpose."

"His own sister. Boy, I wonder what would happen if I ever turned up pregnant?"

"I hope there's no danger."

"You kidding? If it did happen, the three wise men wouldn't be far behind."

Kiki laughed, reached over and touched Camilla's cheek. "You really are precious . . . I think I may take you home with me."

"Suits me. But what did happen? I mean, about the baby? Where did you go?"

"I was up at Ole Miss, and by the time the spring term was over I was beginning to show. I knew if I came back here, Tom would pitch a fit, and I guess I was still a bit afraid of him then. So I went to live with some friends that summer. They didn't have much money at the time, and I wore out my welcome there . . ." She looked off, then back at the baby's grave. There were tears in her eyes. "I didn't have any money, and I wasn't . . . wasn't having an easy time. Tom, of course, had found out by then. I came back here hoping he'd gotten over his anger."

"And he hadn't?"

"No. I was expecting Ouida to be here to help me out with him. She would have, but her mother had taken sick, and she'd gone up there and taken you kids with her. I wouldn't have come back. But something was wrong, and I knew I wasn't going to be able to take care of myself. I came back on my knees to ask for help. It was the only time in my life I ever begged anyone for anything. I begged him just to let me stay until the baby was born—to stay in my own house."

"He wouldn't let you?" Camilla asked, knowing the answer.

"No. I caught a ride out here. It was about dark when I got here. There was no one home. I was about to go down to Lavina's house. Then Tom came home. He still had some woman's lipstick on his shirt collar!" she said. "Maybe I shouldn't tell you this?"

"Yes!" Camilla shouted, surprising herself. "Yes. I want to know."

"He called me a lot of dirty names and told me to leave—to go find the man that did it—if I knew which man did it, he said. He *knew* who the father of the baby was—"

"Why? I mean, didn't he care? The father of the baby?"

"He never knew. They'd been cutting timber here on the place the year before, and he was a young sawmill worker, saving up money to go to college. I . . . We fell in love. When Tom found out, he had him fired and ran him off. A sawmill worker wasn't good enough for his little sister. He never knew about the baby."

"I'm sorry. I really am," Camilla said. "I hope you know that."

"Then, that night, when I had no place else to go, when I knew there was something wrong—I was having so much trouble with the baby—I came back and asked him to help me. I got down on my knees right there in the house and begged him. I begged him to take me into a house that was as much mine as it was his. It sounds silly now, to say that I got down on my knees and begged him. But I did. He pulled off his belt and whipped me. Right there in the hall. Then he slapped me, walked me out on the porch and pushed me down the steps. He swore he would kill me if he ever saw me again—"

"My God!"

"So I left. Mama was staying up at Aunt Iola's, and I couldn't go up there and face them. I didn't have a dime in my pocket and no place to go. My child was born that night, between here and town. These old negroes found us, they worked for Old Man Goodwin—"

"Lavina told us about that. I hate that son of a bitching Tom Kantwith!"

"Please, Camilla, I don't want you—"

"No. You please. I've hated the bastard a long time."

"Anyway, they found us and got Lavina. They never told. At least, not all of it. Oh, Tom knows. How could he not know? But they spared me the final shame. Of that I have always been grateful. Those old negroes were frightened as I was. Old Man Goodwin took me to the hospital in Greenwood and took care of burying the baby, here. He was a good old man."

"I always thought he was an old grouch. Guess I was wrong about that."

"He hardly knew me before that. But he helped me. And later he gave me money to go away. Too bad, I've often thought, I didn't go to him in the first place, but I didn't know him. Human kindness is oftentimes disguised in some mighty strange packages."

"And they never told anyone, not even Lavina."

"No. Stovall was the name of the old negro couple that worked for Old Man Goodwin. What they did for me, Camilla, was something that all the money in the world couldn't buy. They offered me a helping hand when there was nothing to gain by it—and a lot to lose. I tried to repay them later, when I was able."

"Tom Kantwith ought to be killed."

"No. Not killed."

"What's going to happen? When—"

"I don't really know what I am going to do when I see him. Maybe I can make him see the difference between himself and those people who helped me when I needed it. Later I tried to repay them. I had Old Man Goodwin give them some money. It was more money than those old negroes had ever seen in their lives. I had dreamed of the time I could do something for them, from that night they found me. I worked hard so that someday I would be able to help them. They, and what they did for me, gave me inspiration to go on, to make something of myself—to make so much money that I could spit in Tom Kantwith's face if I wanted to. But you can't repay kindness with money, Camilla. 'We was just doing our Christian duty towards you,' that was what old Mrs. Stovall wrote to me once on a Christmas card."

"Where did you go? After you got well?"

"Where did I go? I went everywhere. First to Memphis. I met a young man there who was in the Navy, a pilot, and married him. He was killed in the war, just before Germany surrendered. By that time, I had been living in Santa Fe, New Mexico, for nearly a year. I'd followed my husband all over the place, from one air base to another and occupied myself with all sorts of silly jobs. That's how I met my second husband, Canton Boles Chislom. He lived in Houston, and I've been there ever since."

"Was he rich? Mr. Chislom?"

"He was rich. Very rich. But I didn't marry him for his money. To be honest, I have asked myself a few times if I'd have married him if he hadn't had any. When I met Canton, I'd already learned there is a big old world out there, a different world from here, and that I could make money of my own. I hadn't *done* it yet, but I knew I could.

"In some ways it is a friendlier world. And in some ways it is harder. For me it was easy, because I had already been down and kicked and picked up again. I was prepared for the best or the worst, so I had a little bit of a head start on it. Out there you don't have people you know to help you along when things get rough, but then you don't have them to hold you back either. I was lucky.

Things went my way. Not at first, but after awhile they did."

"I can't wait to get away from here."

"I know."

"Do you really think I could do it? I mean, go away from here and make something of myself, on my own?"

"You don't have to do it on your own. You've got this very rich aunt who has always wanted a daughter . . . always wanted children."

"You didn't have . . . don't have any children?"

"No. No children." She stared at the grave. "Just that one. My husband left me two nephews that we helped raise, but they're grown and starting families of their own. I don't have anyone, Camilla. I was happier with Canton than anyone has a right to be, but since he died . . . I miss him. And I'm very lonely without . . ." There were tears in her eyes.

"Don't cry," Camilla said, reaching out for her.

"I won't. What a wonderful thing it is to come here, finally, to this spot and discover you—"

"Hello!" The voice came from up the slope. They stood up."

"There's a truck up at the church," Camilla said.

"Good. I was expecting them. I ordered a marker for the baby's grave. But I'm going to have them take it back. I think the one your mother put here is just fine, don't you? And it was put here with love. I think we should leave it alone . . ."

15

At The Kit Kat Klub

Mavis Patton's Kit Kat Klub was just west of the Carroll County line on the Vaiden road. It was a two story cottage with a deep sloping roof, looking somewhat as if it had gotten misplaced from a Bavarian forest, sitting back from the road in a stand of pine trees and fronted by a gravel parking lot. The large front room served as the bar and restaurant, and directly behind that was a very large, deep room where dances were often held on weekend nights, and for other special occasions. Upstairs were Mavis' living quarters, two bedrooms, a sitting room, and a bath. Off to the side of the barroom, there was a long, narrow kitchen where a short black woman of ample proportions named Minnie Lee held forth, and if Tom Kantwith was ever totally correct about one thing in his life, it was in his contention that Minnie Lee made the best hamburgers in the state of Mississippi. In fact, it was Minnie Lee's cooking that gave the Kit Kat Klub a veneer of respectability and separated it in people's minds from the two jukejoints across the road and the seedy nightclub and attached motel half a mile up the hill.

When Tom pulled into the parking lot and drove around to the back and parked his car in the usual place—why he bothered to conceal his car at the rear of the building was more than Minnie Lee had ever figured out, since everyone who knew anything knew he spent more time there than he did at home anyway—the cook was staring out the window.

What she was staring at was a man nearly seven feet tall, blue-black in color, with shoulders half as wide as a pickup truck, arms as big as fenceposts, and a waist and hips not much larger than Minnie's upper arms. His head, which was no wider than his neck and seemed to come to a rounded point on top, which put Minnie Lee in mind of a giant penis, was shaved. His name was Jetty Tules, and Minnie Lee was so mortally afraid of him that it was difficult for her to get her work done and keep an eye on his whereabouts at the same time.

Mavis Patton, red-haired, small in stature, with a full figure, came into the kitchen when she heard Tom's car pull up, and saw that Minnie Lee still had not brought in the wash, hanging on the line from the day before.

"Minnie Lee, goddamnit, you gonna leave that wash out there until it rots?"

"I ain't stepping out of this house, long as you got that bluegum nigger out there working in that yard."

"That is just about the craziest thing I ever heard of. What do you think he's going to do to you? You too fat to rape."

"Shows how much some folks know. It's a known fact, one of them bluegum niggers bite you, it the same as having a rattlesnake bite you. One and the same thing."

"I never heard of anything so crazy in my life . . . Tom, you ever heard of anything as crazy as that?" Mavis asked, as he came in the back door.

"Crazy as what? Have to be pretty damn crazy to beat trying to carry on a conversation with that woman my son married."

"Minnie Lee has got this cockeyed idea that Jetty Tules will *bite* her if she goes out in the yard to get that wash in."

"Same as being bit by a rattlesnake."

Tom looked out the window. "Ain't that that Guda nigger old Mr. Brass Palmertree brought back with him from Georgia?"

"I hired him to clean up the mess around this house before the briers and Johnson grass and honeysuckle vines take over everything."

"I sure wouldn't want to get in a fight with that bastard. You see the size the arms on him?"

"I ain't studying arms," Minnie Lee said. "Them two little pointy teeth is my main concern."

"What little pointy teeth?" Tom asked. He rather liked Minnie Lee. He also knew that there was no way Mavis could make her go out to get in the wash if she had her mind made up not to.

"He got two little pointy teeth, just like a rattlesnake."

"Oh, for Christ's sake. Did you feed him something to eat?"

"Made him four hamburgers and put them out on the back porch in a tin plate with a R. C. Cola."

"Well, I never heard of anything so stupid in my life. There's a whole bunch like him lives down round Belzona."

"Uh huh. You ain't seen me going to Belzona, is you?"

"How about seeing if you can't whip up me a couple of those hamburgers with cheese?" Tom said and went into the barroom.

When Tom had eaten his hamburgers, he went up to Mavis' living quarters and went to sleep. He had just nodded off when the jukebox blasted on, with some man on it yelling about somebody getting in the kitchen and rattling pots and pans, causing him to sit bolt upright on the peach colored velvet spread.

Mavis swore. She'd just served beers to Bud, Bevo Harvey, and Progress Whittal, who'd walked in not five minutes after Tom went up to take his nap. She'd gone into the hallway to answer the telephone when Bevo put a quarter in the box and turned up the sound.

"Turn down that goddamn jukebox, Bevo, so I can hear what it is Christine Box has got to say on this telephone."

Bevo turned it down, but not much. The man was now singing about a one-eyed cat looking through a seafood door.

"Bevo, I am going to come out there and unplug that goddamn thing if you don't turn it down. Now turn the fucker down!"

She turned her attention back to the telephone. "Now, what was you saying about your Aunt Beth Ward, Christine? She was in the bank and what?"

"Tell old Christine to bring that hot box of hers on down here!" Bevo yelled and laughed at his own pun, which made Bud a bit nervous. He was pretty sure that his father was upstairs, since his car was parked out back, and Tom had never allowed him to come to the Kit Kat Klub, telling him way back when he was in high school that he could do his tomcatting at any of the other county line joints, but Mavis Patton's place was off limits. Bud wasn't sure but what it was still off limits, and except for the few times he'd seen her on the streets of Bolatusha, the closest he'd ever gotten to Mavis was when she'd served him the beer he was holding in his hand. He was staring at the large poster of a smiling woman holding up a bottle of Coca Cola that was nailed up on the wall next to the window across the bar. Somebody had smashed a fly right on one of her big white teeth.

"Come on, Bud! Wake your lazy ass up and let me beat you at this King Pin game," Bevo said, slapping him on the shoulder. Progress had already staked out one of the pinball machines. Mavis looked around the corner and scowled at Bevo.

"You already told me your Aunt Beth Ward is the treasurer of the South Bolatusha Pentecostal Church, Christine. Get back to what it was she saw in the bank—"

"Lordee! Look at the built on that nigger out yonder!" Bevo shouted, looking out the window at Jetty Tules.

"Hang on a minute, Christine," Mavis said, let the phone dangle, and stepped into the barroom. She was a proud woman, and most of what she was proud of was that hers was the only place within fifty miles where, as she put it, a decent woman could stop in and have herself a bottle of beer, or that a man could bring his wife with him. Bevo was beginning to bruise her pride.

"Let me tell you something, Bevo Harvey. Christine Box is a friend of mine, and she's a married woman, and as far as I know there ain't nobody around who knows what she's got that is hot and what ain't, you get what I'm saying?"

"I didn't mean nothing by it. Just trying to have a little fun. Hell."

"You keep on running your mouth like you been doing, and you're going to get a lot closer look at Jetty Tule's arms than you want, hear me?"

"What in the hell is going on down here?" Tom asked, walking down from the living quarters.

"See if you can put a lid on this ass your son drug in here. Christine Box is on the phone with something important to tell me," Mavis said, and went back to the telephone.

"Hey, Daddy! Never expected to run into you here," Bud said, trying but too nervous to smile.

"The hell you didn't," Tom said, walking around to the cooler and digging out a bottle of Jax.

"Howdy, Mr. Kantwith."

"Progress. Bud, shouldn't you be home looking after that woman?" Tom said.

"What woman is that, Daddy?"

"Well, I hope to hell you've only married one of them. Go on home and take her for a ride or something, and get her out of your mama's hair for awhile."

"Sure, uh, Daddy?" Bud stood up and was backing toward the door."

"What?"

"Progress would like to take Camilla over to that function at the high school tonight, if it's okay with you?"

Tom thought about it for a minute. "I don't care," he said. "But I think we better leave that up to your mama to decide. Now you boys run along."

Tom watched them leave, Bevo reluctantly, and took a seat at the table next to the jukebox. He reached behind the machine and cut the volume down to silence. Mavis hung up the phone, crossed the room, and joined Tom, a perplexed look on her face. Tom knew better than question her; she would tell him what was bothering her in her own good time. She reached across the table and took his hand.

"Mama called me again this morning," she said. "Wanted to know if I could come up there and visit her. She's lonely up there in that old folks' home."

"Weren't you just up there yesterday?"

"Yeah. She wants to come home, come back here. Tears me up every time she calls on that phone and cries like that. But I just can't take care of her, with her down like she is."

"You could hire a nurse, somebody to look after her," Tom said. They'd had this same conversation a dozen times since Mavis had put her mother in the nursing home, back in the winter.

"She's just going to keep getting worse. Doctors say she is just going to keep getting worse. That bastard brother of mine, with his fine home in Tuscaloosa, you think he'd call her ever now and then, or even send her a five cent postcard? No, not him . . . I miss her, too. You live with somebody thirty-odd years, you get used to them. Lord! She was a card in her day, wasn't she a card, Tom?"

"Mrs. Patton was one spry old gal."

"Weren't she, though! Come down here on a Saturday night and dance right along with the kids. Out dance them all! Then she had to go and have that old stroke. Don't seem fair, a woman likes to have a good time like her has to go and have a stroke like that. Just tears me up every time I go up there and see her lying there in that hospital bed in that tiny little old green room. Said last night she wanted me to buy her a bottle of that Iron-Aid and bring it to her."

"Iron-Aid? That the stuff them Germans make up there in Kilmichael, back of the drugstore? What does she do with it?"

"I think she drinks it."

"Drinks it? I thought it was for cuts and wasp stings and things?"

"May be, but I swear she drinks it. She can go through a bottle in no time. You know how she feels about whiskey, but I'll bet you a dollar to nothing that stuff is at least a hundred proof."

"Well, hell, it may be poison to drink."

"If it is, it ain't hurt her none. Course, I'm not sure she drinks it, but I don't know what else she would do with so *much* of it. I never saw her drink it—"

"You said that was Christine on the phone."

"Yeah." She still wasn't ready to tell him what was on her mind.

"Bates still off working on that pipeline?"

"Yeah, and she's still bitching about it. Says with him gone all the time, it's like not even having no husband. Told her I've known all my life what that's like. Told her hell, she didn't know when she was well off, long as he's sending her all that money. Ain't that the truth?"

"I don't know. Mavis . . ."

"Don't mind me, just feeling sorry for myself on account of Mama, you know? Makes me start in wondering what's going to happen when I get to be an old lady like that, and come down with a stroke and end up in some old folks' home. It's something you have to think about, sooner or later."

"Honey, you got a few years before you have to start thinking about something like that. Any case, you won't be a *poor* old lady, you know that. You know I'm about ready to call in my chips, and when I do I want you to sell this place."

"And do what? I'd be lost without this place to run."

"Do whatever you want to do. Hell, you know all that land of mine is going to be worth a fortune, more money than you could ever spend."

"I got all the money I want to spend now, Tom"

"Hell, I'm talking about *real* money. Rich! And I ain't talking about five years from now, either. Soon as we get Perce in the ground and all, I'm going to start making some calls. I think the time has come for me to make my move, let certain folks know what I have. I told you some outfit out of Texas has already picked up the scent and bought three pieces of land here in the last month. That's the proof right there, if I needed more."

"You still think Old Man Goodwin is up to something?"

"Damn right I do. I went over there twice to see him today, and both times that Black girl said he was out on bank business. Now what kind of bank business could be so important that he'd break an appointment with the best customer he's got?"

"What time was you over there? At the bank?"

"Eleven o'clock. And a little while ago."

"He was in the bank at dinnertime. When the hearse come through town with Perce, he was sitting in the bank right after that," Mavis said.

"How do you know that?"

"Christine. You know old Miss Beth Ward?"

Tom nodded.

"Well, she's Christine's aunt on her daddy's side, and she is the treasurer of the South Bolatusha Pentecostal Church? Well, she watched them come through with Perce and then went right straight in the bank, and Old Man Goodwin was sitting there just as big as day at his desk."

Tom knew there was more to the story. He also knew that there was no way in the world that Mavis could be hurried when she had something to tell.

"Miss Beth Ward was making a deposit of yesterday's collection, and told Christine that while she was standing there and Old Man Goodwin was sitting back at his desk, this real dressed up, stuck up looking woman walked in—just like she owned the bank, Miss Beth Ward said. And said she walked right straight back to Old Man Goodwin's desk, carrying one of the little business suitcases and shook his hand. Then they went into that back office that was the old man's and shut the door. Miss Beth said Old Man Goodwin acted real nervous."

"Who was the woman?" Tom asked.

"Let me get to that part. After a little while, they come out and got into a Cadillac car—Miss Beth said it was about the prettiest car she ever saw in her life—and drove off. She'd already come out of the bank and was standing right there on the sidewalk so close to that car she could reach out and touch it, and said that this woman and Old Man Goodwin were laughing and talking to beat the band. Now here's the good part. That car had Texas license plates on it, and on the side window it had this little bitty blue and white sticker that said Houston Hunt Club on it."

"Wonder who in the hell that could of been?"

"Miss Beth Ward said she *knew* who it was, and she'd of known her if she'd of run into her in the middle of the State Fair, and that she walked by Old Man Goodwin's house about ten minutes later, and that car was parked right there in his driveway."

"Well, goddamn, Mavis! Who was it?"

"Well, she could of been mistaken. Miss Beth Ward is getting on."

"Who did she think it was."

"She said she knew who it was. She said it was your sister!"

Tom choked on his beer. "The hell you say! Oh, hell no. She must of been mistaken."

"Well, I'm just telling you what Christine said Miss Beth Ward said. Said that she'd know Kiki Kantwith in the middle of the State Fair, and even with her hair dyed blonde."

"That's not possible . . . Texas license plates?"

"That's exactly what she said. And Houston Hunt Club on that little bitty sticker in the side window. On the driver's side."

"Well, even if it was her, what would she be doing with Donald Goodwin? It don't make any sense."

"I'm just telling you what she said."

"Texas?"

"And that little sticker—"

"I know," he said, standing up.

"Where are you going?"

"To see Donald Goodwin."

"The bank will be closed, time you get there."

"Then I'll see the bastard at his house or wherever I find him." Mavis watched him rush through the kitchen and out the door. He almost ran over Jetty Tules, backing up, and spewed gravel all over the front of the Kit Kat Klub.

"Well, goddamn, Tom. I just two weeks ago paid fifty dollars for that load of gravel . . ."

"Who sot fire to his pants?" Minnie Lee asked.

"I think I just put a bee in his bonnet. Yes, I think I did. I always knew that sister of his would come back on him one of these days. Ain't a Kantwith that ever lived you can cross and get by with."

"You still aiming on getting shut of him?" Minnie Lee asked.

"Oh, one of these days. When I ain't got nothing better to do."

"He ain't never gonna marry you. You *know* that."

"Hell, Minnie Lee, I never wanted to marry him. No, I never did. If there is one woman in the world that I feel sorry for, it is the woman he's married to. Like I always said, Tom is a good man to have around. As long as he's married to somebody else."

16

The Other Kantwiths

Having left Camilla at the church yard with Kiki, Ouida took the path through the woods back to the house. Lavina saw her coming and was waiting for her on the back porch.

"Whole lotta mess going on in this house," she said. "Them kinfolks from down to Attala County showed up, and they took up on one side of the parlor and that old woman with her boys on the other side, and the whole bunch sitting in there seeing who can outstare who and not saying a word. Hazel running around here saying she's sick of this and she's sick of that, and whining and carrying on cause Bud ain't come home yet until I'm plumb sick of her. That soldier come out here a while, but I sent him down to the store to get a cold drink on account of I didn't want him in my way, and he don't know no better than try to be friendly to that bunch in the parlor—"

Lavina had been speaking so rapidly that she had to pause to catch her breath. "Or worse than that get trapped by Hazel carrying on about Chicago this and Memphis that and how *country* and all it is around here. That woman could drive a Holiness preacher to take up with the devil—"

Ouida was about to tell Lavina to calm down when Hazel opened the kitchen screen door and squealed: "I heard that! And I don't like people talking about me behind my back. I especially don't like no hired help talking about me behind my back. At least where I come from the hired help knows its place!"

Barely holding back a temper that had surfaced only a very few times in her entire life, Ouida turned on Hazel and spoke slowly and precisely: "Hazel, we do not look upon anyone in this household as hired help. I want you to understand that, because I hope I never have to remind you of it again. I do not know precisely what your problem is, but you've done nothing but make a nuisance of yourself since you've been here. Now what I want you to do is go to your room or go to the side garden or go anywhere you want, but stay out of the kitchen and leave Lavina alone. Now would you please do that?"

Before she turned and flounced off, Hazel looked from Lavina to Ouida with a smug look on her face and said: "You may not know it, but I know a lot more about things around here than you think I do."

She left Ouida and Lavina staring at each other. "Now what do you suppose she meant by that?" Ouida asked.

Lavina shrugged. "Sure glad she ain't no kin of mine. Even by marriage. You ought to told her to stay away from Camilla, too. The sight of her drives that child crazy and makes her start in fussing too."

"I've come to a realization about Camilla today. It was there all the time, I guess. But you pointed out that I haven't taken the time to—"

"Never mind what I said this morning. I was mad and talking out of turn," Lavina apologized.

"No. You were right. The last couple of years, since I learned that Perce was dead, I haven't been paying the attention I should have to Camilla. Do you know there are girls her age that she went to school with who have babies?"

"Lots of girls her age got babies."

"Yes. She has nearly grown up, and I never even noticed."

"Is that a fact?" Lavina asked with a modicum of sarcasm and a gleam of joy in her eyes.

"Maybe I never noticed because it took me so long to mature myself. Then I saw something today that made me realize a few things about myself and a little about Camilla, and maybe more about you. The whole day has been like looking in mirrors."

"I think I know what you mean about looking in mirrors and maybe I don't. I just hope that Hazel ain't snooping around here someplace listening, cause she'd report you as crazy. What did you see that cleared up your head like that?"

"I saw my daughter suffering because she's becoming a woman and there's been no one to show her how. You made me do that. I sat out there in that wisteria arbor and saw her whole life laid out in front of her. Or tried to. But all I really saw was my own life. I went from a father who was nice enough—but to tell the truth he sent me to college only because he was afraid that I was too much of a little ole mouse to ever catch a husband and figured the only way I'd ever get on in life was to teach school. I went from him to a husband. Do you know what the word *husband* means, Lavina?"

"Means the man you marry."

"It means that, but in olden days it meant the master of the household. That is exactly what it meant, master of the household. There didn't even have to be a *wife* in the household for there to be a husband. The husband was just the master, period."

Lavina didn't even have to think about her next statement: "Still means that in lots of folks' houses. Maybe most."

"Not in yours. Henry doesn't master your house. And you don't either."

"That's a fact. We got equal say. Some things he's got more to say about, and some things I got the most say. It works out about even."

"I don't think it will ever work out anything near even in this house. When I looked at Camilla out there, I was just seeing myself. But I saw something else. I saw that she would never in a thousand years put up with my life, with the life I've lived with Tom."

"You could borrow crop money on that," Lavina said.

"I saw that, and I was scared. Scared for her. I was. Then, after they brought Perce home, I walked in the parlor, and I saw Tom standing there staring at the coffin, and you know what I saw? Lavina, I saw Tom through Camilla's eyes. Yes, I did. And I spoke up to him. I told him to leave her alone. I've asked him to do and not to do in the past, but today was the first time I ever *told* him to do."

"You scared when you done that?"

"No," Ouida said, surprised at the realization that she had not been. "No, I wasn't."

"Then you did do some seeing. Camilla ain't scared of him.

She ain't never been," Lavina said.

"Then I saw Kiki over at the church, and I listened to her talk. Remember how we always thought she was just pretty and sassy and spoiled. What we didn't give her credit for was being stubborn and smart enough not to settle for anything less than she expected out of life."

"Maybe you didn't. My opinion that child was born with the guts to get what she had coming to her. Just like Camilla."

"Yes. That was what else I saw today. I saw myself in her, but the important thing I saw was that she could never see herself in me. She will become the woman she wants to be, and there is not one thing I could do to stop her, even if I wanted to. And try as he may, Tom won't have any more to say about it than I will. Now I better go see about those folks in the parlor."

"That's a fact," Lavina said, a smile playing at her lips.

The folks in the parlor were just as Lavina had described them; the Attala Kantwiths seated on one side, Aunt Iola and her nephews on the other, and a heavy silence hanging between them. Bart Kantwith, Tom's cousin, was a tall, thin man, wearing freshly laundered and pressed overalls and a work shirt, and a fringe of sand colored hair circling his bald dome. Seated next to him was his wife, Jesse—she had been a Gibson from down around McAdams—and flanking them were two of their three daughters, Bobbie Ann and Sue, sisters to Willa Kant, nee, Willadeen. Bobbie Ann's little boy, Jesse Lee, going on eight and as pretty as a little girl with his bright blue eyes and mass of black curly hair, was trying to hide behind his mother's chair.

They all nodded when Ouida entered the room and greeted them. Then Bart nodded toward the coffin and said, "Well, Ouida, it looks like we Kantwiths are dying out. I'm the last of my branch to carry the name—the boy there's a Tatterby—come out from behind there son and say hello to your Cousin Ouida—and I guess you just got the one left, ain't it?"

"Yes," Ouida answered. "Bud. How are you, Jesse? I heard you were sick back in the winter."

"Oh, I was down there awhile with some heart trouble, but I been coming along fine since I changed doctors."

"How are you girls?" Ouida asked. "I don't see you often

enough to remember which one of you is Bobbie Ann and which is Sue."

"I'm Bobbie Ann," said Bobbie Ann, "And she's Sue. This is my boy, Jesse Lee. I guess you heard me and Wilson got a divorce?"

"Willadeen ain't here," said Sue. "She's a movie star in Hollywood. You must of heard about that?"

"Now Sue, I told you not to go talking about Willadeen and Hollywood and all, the first thing off," Bart said, but without much conviction.

"Yes, I heard," Ouida replied.

"She just finished her second film—that the way they call movies out there, films—but it ain't a musical," Sue added.

"Ouida, I sure am sorry about your boy, there," Jesse said. "I really am. I just don't know if I could stand it if I was in your place."

"She's about to get married to a stunt man." That was Sue again.

"Personally, I don't see why she'd go and marry one of them. I was her I'd get me that Guy Madison. Or that Tab Hunter we saw in that movie took place on that island," Bobbie Ann said. For the past several months, since her divorce from Wilson, she'd bombarded Willa Kant with letters pleading to be allowed to bring Jesse Lee and move to Hollywood herself.

"What is a stunt man?" Ouida asked for the want of anything better to say.

"That's a person falls off buildings and horses and things," Sue answered. "You see the star in the movies fall off a horse or something, that ain't the real person. That's a stunt man."

"Oh."

"It's a dangerous job, and they make lots of money, Willadeen says."

"Don't make the money a real movie star makes though," Bobbie Ann added. "I was her I'd latch onto me a real movie star."

"Next *film* she is going to make is another musical with that Gene Kelly," said Sue.

"He'll do," said Bobbie Ann, "but not like that Guy Madison."

"I wish you'd just be quiet about that Guy Madison," Jesse pleaded."This ain't the time to be discussing Guy Madison. I don't even know who Guy Madison is."

"Hush, Bobbie Ann," Bart ordered. "How is Tom getting along, Ouida?"

"He's fine. He had to go over to town. Should be home soon."

"You tell him we're sorry we missed him. And how we feel about the boy."

"I will," Ouida replied, wondering how they felt about the boy.

"Oh, Miss Maidee Morgan? She said us be sure and get your recipe for them hot cucumber preserves like you sent her when she was down sick. She said she never tasted anything so good in her life and thinks that is what made her get up on her feet again," Sue said.

"I will. Poor Miss Maidee. We taught school together. A long time ago at Green Grove."

"I never knew you used to be a schoolteacher," Bobbie Ann said.

"Of course she did," Jesse replied. "She went to Blue Mountain!"

"I was going to study to be a schoolteacher. Before I met Wilson," Bobbie Ann said, as Aunt Iola cleared her throat with a loud feline growl.

"Sue, why don't you run back to the kitchen and get that recipe from Lavina. The kitchen is just straight down the hall. Maybe the rest of us should go out on the porch. It's cool out there this time of the day."

Bart stood up, nodded at the coffin again, then at Aunt Iola, West, and Weir in turn and followed Ouida out the door. Single file, the others followed, with Jesse Lee hanging close to his mother.

As Bobbie Ann closed the door, Aunt Iola, without moving her eyes from the spot where they'd been fixed on the opposite wall for the past half hour said: "I never saw such a pack of damn fools in my life."

"They're kin," West said.

"Not close," Weir replied.

"Close enough," Aunt Iola muttered under her breath.

Out in the hallway, Bart glanced around. "I always say this branch of the Kantwiths got the best of the deal every time I see this house. You know, when Isaac and Grandpa Barton had their falling out."

It was a subject Ouida had been sure would come up before they left—and surely they were leaving?—and one she'd long grown tired of hearing about.

"This house was built later," Ouida said. "By Tom's father, Robert. The house that Isaac and Barton built is the one Aunt Iola lives in with the boys."

"Yes, but Isaac snatched all the money and left it to Robert," Bart said.

"I wouldn't know about that," Ouida replied. "All that was forty years before I married into this family. I hope you all will be coming back up for the funeral services. It's at two o'clock tomorrow." She opened the front door and led them out onto the porch.

"No, don't guess we will. When you're a poor farmer like me the fields won't wait on you. You tell Tom we're sorry we missed him."

"I will," Ouida replied, as Sue came rushing out of the house.

"That Lavina is the nicest old colored woman. You know what she done? She asked me to write to Willadeen and get her to personally autograph a picture for her.

Yes, Ouida could imagine Lavina doing that as she rushed Sue out of the kitchen.

"Best be going now," Bart said.

"You all come and see us now, hear?" Jesse said, taking the steps like a tightwire walker, balancing her bulk first on one foot and then on the other.

Ouida remained at the top of the steps and watched the five of them pile into an off color old Ford. She was still standing there when Kiki and Camilla drove past the store and up toward the house.

17

The May Queen Candidate

Nearly an hour later Camilla, having helped Kiki unpack, walked out on the front porch and took a seat in the swing. It was her favorite time of the day, when the big red ball sun was sliding toward the treetops across Bogue Chitto Bottom.

It was what she thought of as her dream time. Normally she would have gotten off the school bus at the store a little while before, walked up to the house and changed into blue jeans, come out onto the porch and think about the day and plan her study routine for the evening.

Today there were other things to think about. Perce was still a nagging ache at the back of her mind, and she still wished fervently that she could attend the May Queen Ball but had decided that she would not mention it to Ouida again. She had asked Kiki to say nothing about it.

She tried to imagine what Houston would be like. She was going there, of that she was sure. Kiki had said so. She would go there and live with Kiki and go to college. And be pretty—Kiki had already shown her a different way to wear her hair that made her look more grown up and less like she was still back in junior high school. And she would be popular and have real boyfriends. Kiki had said that was so, also.

And she would learn to say "piss off" just like Kiki had said to Hazel. Hazel had invited herself into Kiki's room while they were unpacking and started pawing through her clothing, asking how much things cost and bragging about all the clothes she had, and a bunch of other silly stuff that no one but a full blown fool would bother mentioning to anyone, until Kiki got tired of listening to her and looked her straight in the eye and said, "Hazel, no one invited you in here. Why don't you just piss off?"

Hazel had acted as if she'd been shot; as if she had never heard the word piss before.

Camilla laughed. She looked at the sun over Bogue Chitto and laughed some more. "Piss off," she said, and liked the sound of it. She'd have to use that one on Progress Whittal. Or Bud, who was driving up and parking his car beside Kiki's Cadillac. She watched as he walked around the car, looking at it, as if he was about to make a cash offer for it.

"Whose car is that?" he asked, coming up the steps. "We saw it this morning at Bevo's daddy's place."

"That car? That Cadillac you're talking about?" Camilla asked, as if there might be a dozen cars parked in the drive.

"Of course I'm talking about that Cadillac with the Texas plates. Some woman got out of it at Harvey's."

"Oh, that car. It belongs to Aunt Kiki. Mrs. Katherine Chislom of Houston, Texas."

"You kidding me? Where did she show up from?"

"I just now told you. Houston, Texas."

"Looks like she ain't doing too bad."

"I'd venture to say she's doing pretty good," Camilla replied, trying to sound as much like Kiki as possible.

"What's she like?"

"Nice. She's taking a nap now. Before supper. And before you ask, she is not your wife's favorite person. And if you want to know where she is, she's wandering around here someplace in a full blown snit. Mama is in the kitchen helping Lavina get some supper on the table, and that soldier is down at the barn looking at some cows or something. Anything else you want to know?"

"If you weren't being such a damned smart aleck, I'd ask you if you wanted to go to that function at the high school tonight."

"Uh huh. Now you're going to join in the choir and start in singing about how nice ole Progress Whittal is. Save your breath."

"Progress is not all that bad. Once you get to know him."

"I know him about as well as I intend to. Tom would like for me to marry him and get to know him a lot better, but that will never happen. Anyway, I'm not old enough to get married."

"I didn't say anything about you marrying him, did I? Good Lord. What do you think I am?"

"I think we both know the answer to that, Bud."

"He really does want to take you to that dance tonight. And I could fix it up. What would it hurt if you just showed up there with him and let him escort you up on the stage? You do want to go, don't you?"

"I don't know if I still do or not. If I thought I wouldn't make a fool of myself by coming in last, maybe. Oh, hell, yes, I'd like to go. But Mama says it wouldn't be right, with Perce in the house and all. I think maybe she's right."

"I think I know how to fix it up for you," Bud said.

"Oh, you do, huh? Well, Mama doesn't even want to hear the subject mentioned again."

"Look, I know I can talk her into it, if you want to go. I'll go get her right now, and we'll just get this matter settled once and for all."

"Hey," she said, as Bud started toward the front door. "Wait a damned minute here. What are you doing this for? What do you get out of it?"

"Nothing. Don't you think I've got any pride? I guess I want my sister to win that thing over them other girls. The way I hear it, that little ole Jeanie Downs thinks she's got the thing won hands down. You don't want that little old squirt to beat you out, do you?"

"That thought doesn't exactly make my heart flutter."

"With me and ole Progress there buying votes for you, there ain't no way she'd win. I'll tell you what else, I'll even get Hazel to loan you one of her new dresses—that pretty yellow one she says you admire so much. You're bound to win, dressed up in that."

"Hazel would have a fit before she'd lend me that dress."

"What dress?" Ouida asked, walking out the front door. "When did you get back, Bud?"

"Just now. Mama, I been thinking . . . And I heard them talking over in town today, and the way I see it, there ain't the first reason why Camilla here shouldn't go to that function at the high school tonight."

"No. It wouldn't be right, with her own brother lying here in his coffin."

"Mama, the least she can do is put in an appearance. Just for a little while. I don't think people would think less of her for just showing up for a little while."

"I am sure people will think better of her for not showing up."

"Mama, please?" Camilla pleaded, again excited at the prospect of attending the May Queen Ball. Even with Progress Whittal.

"No."

"Mama, please let me go?"

"Camilla, it just does not seem right to me."

"Mama? Please let me go, Mama? I know darn well I won't win, but at least let me go there and be seen as *something* in that old school for once? It's the only chance I've ever had."

"That's the spirit. And I'll bet she wins it, too," Bud said.

Ouida stared at Camilla for several moments, thinking about a possibility that she would not have considered only a few hours before. "Are you sure you feel it's the right thing, Camilla? Deep in your heart?"

"I don't know, honestly. How would Perce feel about it, you reckon?"

"That is just what I was thinking about. A lot of things I've seen and heard don't seem right to me, but maybe I'm not always right myself."

"You think he'd want me to go?"

"When I think about it," Ouida replied, "the way you felt about Perce and the way he felt about you, I think maybe he would have wanted you to go. I guess you better start prettying yourself up. But eat you some supper first. I don't want you getting sick—"

"Mama!" Camilla jumped out of the swing and hugged Ouida, then rushed into the house.

"Bud, you better go in the kitchen, too. Hazel is eating her supper at the table by herself and not liking it one bit."

"Yeah, and I got to talk her into loaning Camilla a dress . . . I guess Kiki Kantwith has come home, huh?"

"She has, and I'm not looking forward to the time your father gets here and finds out," Ouida replied.

"Doesn't he know?"

"No. I just found out she was coming this morning, myself.

And I never found the time to tell him, with all that's been going on around here today."

"What do you think he's going to say?"

"I haven't the slightest idea," Ouida replied.

"I'll bet there is going to be some hell to pay," Bud said, going into the house.

"Yes," Ouida said to herself. "But what I wonder is, who is going to be the one to pay it?"

Half an hour later, wearing Hazel's yellow chiffon dress, Camilla knocked on Kiki's bedroom door. Kiki was up, dressed, and combing her hair.

"Who is it?" she asked.

"It's me, Camilla!"

"Come on in."

Kiki turned and stared at her. "What in God's name is that you've got on? Aren't you a little old to be playing dress up?"

"It's Hazel's. Bud talked Mama into letting me go to the May Queen Ball, and even made Hazel loan me this dress. Isn't that something? I'm going to get to go, after all. Mama thought it over and decided it was what Perce would have wanted, for me to go in spite of, you know—"

"Now slow down a minute. I think that it's wonderful that Ouida decided to let you go, but who are you going with? Who's your escort?"

"Oh, ole Progress. But that's better than having to walk up on the stage by myself, I guess."

"I think I just got a whiff of rotten fish. First of all, sweetheart, you can't go anyplace dressed like that. That dress is just plain tacky, not to mention that it is about three sizes too big for you."

"I was thinking I could stuff some cotton in my bra."

"No way. Besides, it would take two baby pigs to fill out the front of that thing. But I think I can solve that problem for you. You know that pink shirtwaist dress you were admiring this afternoon? I think, if we took the hem up about four or so inches, it would be perfect. You wouldn't be the flashiest looking girl there, but you'd win the class contest hands down. You game?"

"Oh, yes. But I don't have time. Bud and Hazel are waiting for me. We have to go way over nearly to the county line and pick

Progress up. He didn't know if Mama would let me go or not, so we have to give him time to get ready."

"Is that a fact? Well, I can certainly fix that up for you, too. Besides, I've been looking forward to meeting my nephew Bud. Now you get out of that thing and comb out your hair. It's still wet anyway. Just keep combing your hair until I get back." With that, Kiki walked out the door and closed it behind herself.

She went to the kitchen first. Lavina was putting food in a basket for her own family's supper. "Where is everyone?" she asked.

"I don't know. I guess they out yonder somewheres waiting on Camilla. I finally got rid of them old people. Had to send them off with enough supper for ten people."

"You going home now?"

"Yes sir! Been one long day for me around here."

"I hope you hear some good news about Jamie."

"I hope so too . . . Miss Kiki?"

"What, Lavina?"

"It sure is good to have you back home."

Kiki hugged the black woman and went looking for Ouida.

She found all three of them, Ouida, Bud, and Hazel, in the living room, where Ouida had talked to Old Man Goodwin earlier that day.

"You must be Bud," Kiki said as she entered the room.

"Aunt Kiki? I sure not would ever recognized you. This is my wife Hazel—"

"We already met," Hazel said and turned away.

"Ouida, Camilla told me about the May Queen contest, that you're letting her go. I think that's wonderful."

"Well, where is she? We got to get a move on," Bud said.

"She's not half ready to go anyplace. Why, her hair is still wet," Kiki said.

"That is just what I was saying. They have to give her time to look presentable," Ouida agreed.

"I tell you what. You have to pick up Progress, I understand, and it has been years since I attended a high school dance—since I was in high school myself, I suppose. I will help Camilla finish dressing, and we'll meet you there."

"Now that sounds like a much better idea to me," Ouida said.

Bud wanted to protest, but could find no real reason to.

They walked Bud and Hazel to the front porch. The soldier, James Lyon Hansen, was seated in the swing.

As Bud and Hazel got in the car to drive off, Kiki looked at the soldier, then at Ouida. Ouida read her mind.

"Well," Kiki said, "what do you think?"

Ouida almost giggled. "You haven't changed a bit, have you? Always up to some devilment."

"What was your name again, young man?"

"Hansen. James Lyon Hansen."

"You know, Kiki, I don't really know if I can be a party to this," Ouida said.

"Be quiet. Of course you can. She's your daughter. James Lyon Hansen, how would you feel about escorting a lovely young lady to a high school dance? I realize you're a bit older, and high school dances may seem a bit silly to you, but you'll never have a prettier date."

"You mean Camilla?" the soldier asked.

"That's who I mean."

"I thought I heard her brother say she had a date."

"Let's just say that she doesn't prefer her date."

"Hey, I'd like it just fine, but I'm supposed to stay here. With the coffin."

"Son, I looked over my boy a great many years, even before you were born. I suppose I can do it now. Anyway, I would like to be by myself with him for a while, without that uniform of yours reminding me of it all," Ouida said.

"Yes, but I have orders," James Lyon protested, weakly.

"Your orders are to comfort the family in whatever way you can, aren't they?" Kiki asked.

"Sure, but—"

"Well, you can best comfort this family by taking Camilla to that dance. We'll go in my car, and I'll even play chauffeur. Now run along and freshen yourself up."

As James Lyon disappeared into the house, Kiki looked at Ouida and laughed. "And I'm going to make damned sure she wins the thing, too."

18

That Evening Sun Goes Down

It was nearly dusk when Henry Lambert came up the dusty road toward his house. He could see Lavina sitting rocking in the shade of the morning glory vines that were strung from the yard to the roof and would shelter one end of the front porch from the hot afternoon sun when full summer came. Without seeing her face or enough of her body to *see* who it was, he knew it was Lavina and not one of his daughters. Done with her work at Miz Ouida's house, she would sit there until it was dark, with supper already on the table for him and the girls. He wished that she wasn't sitting there where she could see him, or that he could slip past her and out to the cowshed without having to tell her yet. But she was waiting for him, and he knew he had to do it; walk right up on the porch and tell her what he found out. Nobody had seen Jamie. Jamie was gone. Not where or why or how. Just gone.

Wearily he mounted the steps, crossed behind his wife, and took a long drink of water from the bucket sitting on the water stand beside the door. Then he struck a match to his pipe, returned to the steps, and sat down.

"You have to walk all the way?" Lavina asked.

"Most of the way back. Bud picked me up over there by Shiloh Church. Got a ride over there with that fellow works for Miz Love. That redheaded man."

"The girls want to go to that play party they having for letting out of school tonight."

"I done told them this morning, they too young to be going

out at night. I told them to stay home."

"They want to go, but I told them no. That pipe stinks."

"Huh," he said and sat smoking his pipe, not looking at her, nor anything else in particular. He knew that she was staring across the fields where the sun was sinking into Bogue Chitto swamp, with her eyes fixed and unemotional, her face set and smooth, hiding the worry and hurt behind it. She turned, slowly and deliberately, and looked at him for a second.

"Shoo them chickens out of the yard. It ain't been ten minutes since I swept it."

Henry got up and chased the chickens out of the yard, swept clean and bordered with brown snuff bottles stuck into the ground up to their necks. He returned to the steps and sat down.

"He ain't there," He said after a moment.

"I know he ain't there."

"How do you know?" Henry turned and asked his wife.

"How I know anything? How I know Sunday when he didn't come home he's not coming back? I know. I feel it, that's how I know. I ask the heart in me, and it answer me back. He ain't coming back, Jamie ain't, it says that. You don't have to tell me he ain't there. I know that," she said, an angry edge to her voice.

"Then what is it I'm supposed to tell you?" Henry asked, feeling hurt and tired.

"Tell me what he done. Tell me who he done it to. Tell me what he suppose to done and who he suppose to done it to. Tell me that."

"I don't know. Everybody I ask say they don't know nothing about Jamie Boy. I asked the Sheriff, and he tells me the truth when he tells me he don't know nothing about Jamie. All I know is that he done something that folks know without knowing what it was."

They sat in silence for a few minutes. Her gaze had returned to the fields, and he stared at his feet, dusty from walking the dirt road.

"Crows gonna peck all your corn out of the ground, you don't build a scarecrow," she said after a moment.

"Jamie going to do it Sunday."

"Jamie has done his last round here. You wait for Jamie to do it, you have a long wait."

"It ain't my fault. You talking like it my fault," he said angrily, remembering the stares in town, folks looking at him and knowing who he was and what he was in town for, looking for his son that had not come home. Remembering the white men standing around in front of the courthouse and feeling them silently asking, "Hey, nigger, what are you doing? You looking for that boy of yours?" Remembering, with pain, wanting to ask where he was, where Jamie had gone and why he'd gone, and being powerless to ask the words.

"You ask anybody where he was?" Lavina asked.

"Matt McNeil, I told you. And colored folks . . . Every colored folk I see, I ask them has they seen him."

"Colored folks," she said with disdain. "How they gonna know? You think they done something to him? You think they sent him away?"

"I thought maybe he talked to somebody, that's what I thought."

"You ask that old Harvey man what happened to Jamie? He sees everything that comes and goes in Bolatusha."

"What am I gonna talk to that white man about?" he asked. They both knew that whenever there was trouble between whites and negroes in Bolatusha, Bevo Harvey's father was either a part of it or certainly found out about it soon enough.

"I go to town, I'll talk to him for sure," Lavina said vehemently.

"What you gonna say to him? Where is my son? What has you white folks done with my son? You gonna ask him that?"

"You don't think I wouldn't ask him that? Jamie is my son. I got a right to know what happened to him."

"I done the best I could, Lavina. I tried to find him, but there weren't the first trace."

"You afraid. You afraid to ask where your own boy is. You afraid somebody will think you acting smart."

"I weren't afraid. Everybody staring at me, knowing I was looking. Everywhere I walk, all over town, somebody was staring at me. They *know* Jamie is gone," he said sadly.

"You afraid to even ask. Don't you think Jamie is afraid? What they done to him, don't you think he was afraid ten times as much as you? To make him leave if he left without saying nothing to us, don't you think he was afraid?"

He looked at the ground where a little jagged ditch had been beaten into the earth by raindrops from the porch roof. At the barn the cows were milling, waiting to be milked. The sound of their bells floated across the early evening silence and echoed in the woods beyond the fields. A fresh breeze from the east followed the shadows across the yard to the porch and cooled his face.

"You ought to come with me, you think you could find out so much," he said after awhile.

"I had work to do. Maybe I will go and maybe I won't. I'll take Miss Kiki with me. Maybe I will find out and maybe I won't, but I won't be afraid to ask. That is for sure," she said.

"You brave sitting there talking about it."

"Brave or not brave, somebody's got a right to know when their boy take off in thin air and nobody to say where he has gone, and you afraid to ask them even if they know." She paused, knowing that Henry believed the worst, that Jamie was probably dead, and still refusing to consider such a possibility herself. "How you know Jamie didn't just haul off and leave?"

"What do you mean, Lavina? You *know* Jamie Boy ain't gonna go running off and not tell us first. Jamie was *run* off."

"That's what I'm saying. If you don't ask nobody what happened to him, how you gonna know what happened? How can you 'spect he is dead without having some proof of it."

"It's happened before," Henry said.

"Yes, and folks *knowed* it. Folks knew by the next morning."

"Times changed. Now they can't get away with that kind of stuff. Now they do it quiet. Nobody ever know."

"*Some*body knows," Lavina said, her voice going to pain.

"I'm tired, woman. Let me rest here a minute before I got to go milk my cows," he pleaded.

"Jamie ain't resting," she said and resumed rocking.

After a few minutes, Henry stood up.

"You gonna milk now?" she asked.

"I better. It be dark soon," he answered and walked across the yard. At the corner he stopped. "Lavina?"

"What?"

"I wish you would keep the girls home tonight. I surely do. It would make me rest a lot easier," he said.

Lavina rocked back and forth in the chair, staring at the rays of the setting sun, like strands of white gold between the trees on the other side of the fields. She held back her tears and hummed: *Shine on mighty river, take away my fears . . .*

At the barn, Henry fed the livestock and waited for the girls to bring the clean milk pails. Neither of them spoke to him, but smiled and went about their chores. He busied himself with the milking until they were finished.

"What's Lavina fixing for supper?" he asked, as they turned the calves in to strip the cows.

"She brought something from up yonder," Maryjane answered. "She just sit on the porch rocking and not even fix no ice tea since she come home."

"You go fix it then."

"You find out what happen to Bubba?" Clarise asked.

"I didn't find out nothing. Ain't nobody saying nothing."

"Bet Bubba don't be coming back here no more," Maryjane said, emphatically. "Bet he long gone from around here. That's what everybody saying at school today."

"Ain't nobody to ask," Henry said, more to himself than to his daughters. He wished the darkness would fall immediately. It embarrassed him to stand before his daughters, helpless to relieve their timid anxiety. He felt guilty, as if it was his fault that Jamie was gone.

"Mama, she gonna set out on that front porch and just sing them old songs til she finds out what happen," Clarise said.

"Mama say you could find out if you wanted to," Maryjane added.

"How I supposed to find out? Who I supposed to ask? I done the best I know how. I ask everybody I knew if they know where Jamie is, and none of them said. Your mama knows I done the best I can," Henry said, wiping an imaginary bead of sweat from his forehead. Darkness was falling now, and down in the meadow a whippoorwill cried. "She knows that."

"Mama say you want to find out bad enough you gotta go ask old Trace McCall," Clarise said.

"Mama says old Trace McCall know everything that happen on account of Miss Maul."

"Your mama knows I ain't spoken to Trace for ten years or

more. What makes her think he gonna tell me anything?"

"Mama just say that is the one sure way of finding out what happen," Maryjane said, matter of factly.

"I start getting messed up with that Trace, then I'll be in some trouble of my own," Henry said. He stared across the darkening landscape for a minute, his eyes searching. "You girls take the milk on back to the house," he said.

"Where are you going?" Clarise asked."

"Never mind. Just do what I say, and don't let me hear about you all going off to that schoolhouse tonight either."

He walked very slowly, his feet tired and blistered, dragging the heavy shoes in the still-hot sand of the path. At the crossing, he walked through the water, wetting his trousers up to the knees, but he didn't pause or seem to notice or even look down at the slow flowing little creek. He wished he had some chewing tobacco left to kill the hunger juices in his mouth. He wished that Lavina wasn't still sitting there on the porch staring at the dark fields, seeing Jamie out there yelling at the mules as he went about his work. "A man do all he can do and be afraid of doing it and be afraid of doing more, what more can he do? Go to the devil, himself, is the last left," he said to the dark tree shadows and heard his voice echo in the deep woods.

Back on the porch, Lavina continued to rock and remember, until the moon came up.

Up at the big house, Ouida played the organ, as she often did when she was alone, played on into the night and said her final goodbyes to her son. She wondered whatever happened to the old Scotch-Irish custom of the wake that brought visitors to the home of the deceased in the time of her youth. But who was there, really, to come and sit up with Perce Kantwith? People were either afraid of Tom or had no use for him. And she had, over the years, gradually come to avoid social gatherings altogether, bonding herself so close to Shadowland that she left no more than four or five times a year now. She had long ago realized and accepted that Lavina was the only real friend she had. And tonight her friend had to confront her own grief.

Ouida knew that Lavina could hear the music of the pump organ down at her house and that she appreciated it. She stopped in mid-song, trying to remember the strange old folk gospel that

Lavina had taught her years before . . . *Shine on, mighty river*—She couldn't remember it. Perhaps it would come to her later.

The song being played at the Bolatusha High School gym was Perez Prado's *Cherry Pink and Apple Blossom White*, which was the cue for the May Queen candidates and their escorts to walk onto the stage.

Three of the girls wore a lot of frills, ruffles, and rhinestones; Camilla, escorted by the uniformed James Lyon Hansen and dressed in the pink silk dress and pearl earrings, her hair pulled back into a chignon, made them look frumpy. She was, as Kiki had predicted, the class act.

Following a rather cumbersome speech about how the funds being raised would go into the new sports facility building project, Vern Hawke, history teacher and assistant basketball coach, finally got around to introducing the candidates and their escorts. Much to her surprise, Camilla got as much applause as Jeanie Downs, if not more. It surprised Jeanie, too. Then Neil Troup explained, once again, that voting was done by money—each penny equaled one vote; a dollar equaled one hundred votes; ten dollars a thousand votes, and so forth; that containers with each candidate's picture on them had been placed in businesses throughout the school district for the past two weeks, and the voting booths, with candidates in attendance, had been open in the gym all evening. Nevertheless, everyone was going to get one more chance to vote.

"Now you fellows get those wallets out of your pockets, and you ladies come on up here and vote for your friends and daughters. Just remember that the money we raise here tonight will go to a good cause—the Bolatusha High School Panthers! Now we will play one more song, and while it is playing will be your last chance to vote for your favorite candidate for May Queen. Just one record now!"

The record on the machine was flipped over to *The St. Louis Blues Mambo*. A few, not many, people came up and put money in the Kerr fruitjars with photographs of the girls taped to them. It seemed to Camilla that the least was going into her jar. But it seemed that there had been as many people milling around her booth all evening as any of the others, if not more. And a lot of the girls made a big fuss over the way she looked. Neil Troup—

who was practically engaged to Alice Jones, was the most handsome boy in school, had made just about all-everything in four sports, and was Camilla's rival for valedictorian—even told her she had pretty ears! Alice Jones looked like she was going to have a litter.

Finally the new "votes" were added to the tally from the voting booths and from the containers gathered from the business places and homerooms.

"Well, folks," said Vern Hawke, "we do have a winner, and in just a moment you will meet the 1954 Bolatusha High School May Queen. But first I would like to thank all of you and tell you that this has been by far the most successful fund raising function of this kind we've had here since I came to Bolatusha twelve years ago and became involved in our efforts to make a better school for you and ours—"

Camilla stopped listening. She was worried—all the girls were. She wondered if she was the only one that saw Jeanie Downs' father come up and stuff a twenty dollar bill in her jar just before the song was over? That was probably the icing on the cake.

She looked down at Aunt Kiki, who was smiling and talking to Old Man Goodwin and his wife—whatever her name was, Camilla was too nervous to remember. She wondered why Kiki was so confident that she would win—so was James Lyon Hansen, who was standing beside her, smiling down at her now, and had immediately, on sight, pushed dreams of Tab Hunter out of the heads of every female student at Bolatusha High School. Except for Alice Jones, who let it be known that her mother would never let *her* go anyplace with a strange soldier.

Vern Hawke came back onto the stage. "And now folks, this is the moment you've all been waiting for. We are going to announce the order of finish and the total votes and tally. As your names are called out, you young ladies come forward and take your positions around the throne. The last name called will be the 1954 Bolatusha High School May Queen!"

There were a few cheers. Bootsie McCoy, the candidate from the junior class, started sniffing. She even cried when the football team lost a game.

"Okay, folks. With 4,992 votes—that is forty nine dollars and ninety-two cents, folks! And in fourth place, is the sophomore candidate, Debbie Sue King! Come on up and take your place, Debbie Sue!" Hawke shouted to the applause.

"Now then. Third . . . No, that would be second runner up. Second runner up, with 5,345 votes—fifty three dollars and forty five cents—is the junior class candidate, Bootsie McCoy!" While everyone applauded Bootsie cried and blew her nose.

"Now folks," said Vern Hawke at his most officious, "we have come down to the wire right here, folks! Will our May Queen for this year be the freshman candidate, Jeanie Downs; or the senior class candidate, Camilla Kantwith? What do you folks think?"

There were a lot of whoops and shouting of both names, before Verne Hawke held up his hands and quieted the crowd. "Okay, folks, first runner up, with a total of 9,112 votes, is the freshman candidate, Jeanie Downs!"

The crowd went wild, whooping and hollering. Jeanie Downs looked like she'd been shot and started sniffing right along with Bootsie McCoy.

"And now folks, with a total of 26,888 votes—and that comes to a grand total of two hundred, sixty eight dollars and eighty-eight cents—is Bolatusha High's 1954 May Queen, Camilla Kantwith!" There was a stunned silence for a moment, after the amount of money was announced, then more cheering than before. Camilla, escorted by James Lyon Hansen, walked to the front of the stage and took a bow. Then Sheriff Matt McNeil handed James the crown, which he placed on her head, leaned over and kissed her lightly on the cheek and there were more howls and cheers from the audience.

Kiki was down front with the Goodwins. They were applauding and waving. Progress Whittal, near the middle of the crowd, was jumping up and down and shouting. He really didn't have sense enough to know when he'd lost. Bud and Hazel were standing next to him, as still and silent as stones. Piss on them, thought Camilla.

And the May Queen, as she walked up the step and sat on the throne (and was tempted to pinch Jeanie Downs on the butt as she brushed past her and really give her something to sniffle about) to have her photograph taken, was thinking: It really is no big thing. I mean, what do you get? A cardboard crown painted silver with some glitter glued to it, a bunch of people yelling at you, and your picture on a whole page in next year's annual. And, besides, Aunt Kiki had paid for it; of that Camilla was sure.

She continued to be rather blasé about the whole thing, until Kiki told her later that she would have won by a landslide anyway, without her help. "I only put in a hundred dollars, sweetheart. I thought that would be more than enough to clinch it for you."

"And I put in ten," James Lyon Hansen said, and quickly apologized: "It was all I could afford."

"You mean I got about a hundred and fifty dollars on my *own*?" Camilla asked.

"Looks like it," Kiki replied. "I certainly don't think Bud and Hazel coughed up much."

Camilla started laughing. For the first time she felt as if she really had won something; that, at last, she really was somebody at Bolatusha High School. She couldn't stop laughing, as people came over—even lined up—to congratulate her. In fact she didn't stop laughing until Neil Troup the all-everything came up and put both arms around her, nodded at James Lyon Hansen, and said, "I guess if that guy can do it, so can I," kissed her on the cheek, and whispered in her ear, "You know, I've always thought you were the cutest girl in school." Then he blushed and walked off back toward Alice Jones, who looked like she'd just kissed a frog's behind.

And while Camilla was taking her bows, with James Lyon Hansen standing on one side and Katherine Chislom on the other, Tom Kantwith walked into the Kit Kat Club, wearing the expression of a man who had just been painfully, perhaps mortally wounded from a blow he didn't see coming.

Instead of going around the bar and getting his own Jax from the cooler, as was his habit, he sat down on one of the stools and propped his elbows in front of him.

Mavis brought him the beer. "Well?" she said. "What hit you?"

"A woman."

"Was she driving a tank, or does she just like to fight?"

"I suspect this one likes a good fight. Would you get me another beer?"

"Your sister?" Mavis asked, opening the beer.

Tom looked up, surprised. "How did you know?"

"Tom, one of your big problems—in fact it is your real big problem—is that you have never given women credit for having any sense. When I heard that your sister was at the bank playing palsy walsy with Donald Goodwin, I never thought she was there because she was after his body when they went in his old man's private office and shut the door. So what'd she do to you."

"Nothing yet. But she's got me between a rock and a hard place."

"By the balls with a downhill drag, huh?" Mavis asked. For some reason she felt a sense of relief; she almost wanted to laugh, knowing that Tom would never forgive her.

"If you want to put it that way."

"What can you do about it?"

"Not a thing, Donald Goodwin says. Either way I move, she can put the squeeze on. Says all these years I been running around here playing the big fish in a small pond, there was a shark over in Houston, Texas, just throwing me bits and scraps, waiting for me to get fat enough to gobble up."

"And the shark was your sister. Kiki?"

"Kiki, hell. Mrs. Chislom. She was married to old man Chislom. You talking Chislom money, you talking up in the millions. Goodwin says old man Chislom taught her everything he knew about his business, and by God if she ain't at least as good at it as he was. And ten times as ruthless, was the way he put it. My own damned sister, Mave."

"Tom, my boy, you have been pussywhipped. And from what I know about you and your sister, you had it coming for a long time, and she was the one to do it. You better go home and pay your respects to the lady."

"I ain't looking forward to that. By God, I still find it hard to believe. Me going around here all these years buying up land, thinking it was floating on a sea of oil—and borrowing money to do it from her the whole fucking time! Can you beat that? She was even directing them Goodwins as to which land to let me buy and which not to let me buy! Now beat that one."

"And there ain't no oil," Mavis said.

"There ain't no oil."

"Then why would she waste her money letting you buy up a bunch of worthless land just to take it away from you? That don't make no sense," Mavis said.

"Natural gas, Mavis. Like down yonder below Pickens? Natural gas. And the experts old man Chislom hired back years ago told him that in another ten, fifteen years, Texas gas is going to start petering out. People in New York City will be heating their homes with Mississippi natural gas. And there's a field under Bogue Chitto twelve miles wide and nearly twenty long. I hold title on almost all of it."

"And she holds title on you?"

"That looks to be about the size of it. Every time I've bought a piece of land, I've had to mortgage the one I bought before. I'm borrowed to the hilt on everything I own. Hell, even Shadowland is mortgaged. Anytime the bank wants to pull the rug, all they have to do is jerk. And you know what?"

"What?"

"She owns the goddamn bank!"

"Well, if I was in your shoes, Tom, I go on home and start in making a few amends you long overdue to make to the lady, before she decides to wipe up Bogue Chitto with your ass."

"Yeah, I guess so," he said, standing.

Mavis couldn't resist. "And Tom, your old lady finally puts you out, I guess you could move in here. It really has been lonely since I had to put Mama in that home."

He threw her a pained expression and went out the door. Mavis wondered if she really would let him move in with her, if it came to that? Probably. But one thing was for damn sure; she'd never marry him.

19

What The Voodoo Woman Knew

Trace McCall, a man as black as the night, lived on the old cut-off road near Mount Hope Freewill Colored Baptist Church and Day School. He lived there in a house that had been owned by his father and by his grandfather before that, with a woman he had brought back from New Orleans nearly forty years before. At the time, the woman had been the subject of a great deal of talk, as she was almost white and spoke no English, only a Louisana French that no one could understand.

It was said that she was the daughter of a voodoo queen, and it was a known fact that she could cast spells and sold gris gris that could catch a lover, get rid of one, bring you money and power, and do a lot of other things that most people didn't want to think about. Trace, as had his father before him, sold bootleg whiskey and ran crap games in his side room.

Some time before Henry reached Trace's house, his approach was signaled by the barking of a dog and Trace's voice telling it to hush. Trace was sitting in the dark on the screenwire enclosed porch. Henry hesitated for a minute at the foot of the steps until he saw the glow of Trace's cigarette in the dark.

"That you, Trace?" he asked.

"It me. Who there?" Trace asked with a voice that bellowed.

"It Henry Lambert."

"Ha. Must be highly important you come to my house after ten years. You come to apologize?"

"No," Henry answered softly, remembering the card game that night ten summers before, when he had caught Trace cheating. There had been a knife fight right on that very same porch.

"I still carrying your scar," Trace said, fingering the long white scar that ran from his temple to his chin. "What make you think I want to invite you up on my porch, carrying your scar?"

"I am sorry about cutting you that time," Henry said. "I truly sorry I had to cut you."

"Then come on in the porch," Trace said.

Henry walked up the steps and onto the porch, stepping on the dog lying there in the dark. The hound snapped at him and commenced barking.

"Be quiet there, Sam, goddamnit. That goddamn dog always laying in the door under folks' feet. You set down there, Henry," he added.

Henry sat down in the chair near the steps. He could barely make out Trace's form across from him in the swing. Trace was a big man, fat with success, but still strong and virile.

"You walk like a tired man," Trace said, after a moment. He shifted his weight, and the swing chains creaked. "You walk up here tired and old."

"I is tired. For sure," Henry said.

"You want a drink of whiskey?"

Henry started to refuse, then thought better. Trace was easily insulted. "I ain't got much money on me," he said, after a moment.

"I ask you do you want a drink. You didn't ask me to sell you one, man," Trace said forcefully.

"I need one, that for sure," Henry said.

"Ha. You ain't been known to drink in ten years."

"I took a few. I ain't bought one in about that long," Henry said, knowing that Trace would be the first person to know if he did. As far as he knew, Trace was the only colored bootlegger in the county.

"Miss Maul!" Trace yelled.

"What?" a woman's voice asked from the dark interior of the house.

"Brang me that bottle of bonded that is open and brang us two glasses to drink it out of."

"Ha!" the woman shouted, her voice slurred with the French accent she never lost. "I know who is there with you."

"That woman see in the dark like a cat," Trace said after a moment.

Almost immediately the woman brought the whiskey and three glasses and poured each of them a drink, neat. She set the bottle on the table at Henry's side and stood at the door, behind him. Now and then she took a sip of her whiskey and giggled to herself.

"This is good whiskey," Henry commented, after awhile.

"Best whiskey can be bought in the state of Mississippi," Trace said. "Even the Sheriff prefer it," he added and roared at his joke.

"Come somebody down the road," the woman said. Henry listened but couldn't hear a sound.

"I don't hear nothing," he said.

"Me and you won't hear them for 'bout five minutes," Trace said. "Miss Maul got ears like a cat too."

"They white mens, by they steps," Miss Maul said.

"How she know that?" Henry asked.

"Miss Maul know everything," Trace answered.

"They ain't coming here," Miss Maul said.

"Where they going?" Henry asked, skeptically.

"On past here," she answered.

They waited, and the forms of three boys moved slowly into view on the road. The dog barked, pushed the screen door open with his body, and rushed into the road.

"Watch out for that dog," a voice shouted, and sounded like that of a white youth.

"Moonlight makes boys ramble," Miss Maul commented.

"Chunk something at that damn hound," another boy shouted, moving away from the dog.

"Git back to your house, nigger dog," the third boy yelled, "'fore I kick the hell out of you."

"Hey, you kick my dog and I hex you the rest of you life, you," Miss Maul shouted back.

"You can't see me!" the boy yelled.

"I sees you, little Jenkins boy. I even sees the freckles on you face, you!" Miss Maul shouted, and the boys whooped and ran. They quickly disappeared around the bend of the road. When their shouts had diminished, Miss Maul returned to her post by the door.

"How you see in the dark like that?" Henry asked.

"I sees everything, I do," Miss Maul said. After a bit she went on: "I see you coming here for something. I see you a tired man looking for a son you can't find. I see your wife singing old grieving songs—"

"What about my son?" Henry asked.

"I see you ain't gonna find him, me. I see you so tired you ready to fall asleep right now on my front door. I see your feet hurt and your heart ache from looking, and I see your Lavina, keeping her grief to herself this whole long day, now saying where is my boy? I see you looking and looking and there ain't no finding. I sees that."

"Miss Maul sees things you and me don't tamper with," Trace said.

"You see so much, maybe you see where my son is at. You see that?" Henry asked.

"Man, she don't have to conjer to see that," Trace said, and Miss Maul giggled, her voice piercing Henry's ears, rising and falling like a winter wind.

"Stop that goddamn laughing and pour the man some more whiskey," Trace said.

"What happened to Jamie?"

"Jamie, he a devil. A real devil," Miss Maul said.

"Anybody can tell you Jamie a good boy," Henry said, turning and trying to see her in the dark. "He do just what I tell him to do. He work in the field like a man."

"Jamie come here Saturday and buy whiskey," Miss Maul said.

"Is that so, Trace?" Henry asked.

"It's a fact."

"*That* the cause of Jamie's trouble," Miss Maul said.

"You so mad at me you never took the time to teach Jamie how to drink his whiskey," Trace said. "Once he got a taste of it, he got big as the world and out of his head."

"What did he do?" Henry asked.

"He bought hisself a whole lot of trouble. He bought hisself more trouble than any nigger wants for two cents. That's what you might say, he bought two cents worth of trouble," Trace answered.

"What's you saying? What is it he done?" Henry asked.

"He spit on a white man, that's what he do," Miss Maul said.

Henry felt his fingers sweating on the glass he held. He stared out into the moonlight and heard himself gasp. A door slammed somewhere, and Jamie was behind it. He was suddenly very tired, exhausted. He let his body sag in the chair. "What made him do that?" he asked.

"Jamie left here on his way to Bolatusha, but one of them crazy Kilmichael niggers come along on his way to Wardsville, and Jamie put out his thumb going that way. He crazy on his first whiskey and not caring where he going. So he went on to Wardsville."

"And got into trouble?"

"A whole lot of trouble. The story come to me this way just today. He went into that service station out there on the highway other side of Wardsville, and went in there and asked the man for a grape drink. He gave the man a dime to pay for it, and the man give him three cents back. You notice I ain't calling the man's name? You know who the man is, and I don't want it coming back to me that you been around saying Trace told me that Mr. So and So done this and Mr. Somebody Else done that—"

"What was done?" Henry asked, fearful to know.

"The man give Jamie three cents back, and Jamie, he say, where my other two cents, you see?" Trace took a sip of his drink and went on. "You know they a lot tougher on niggers down in Wardsville than they are over at Bolatusha. So the man says to Jamie, he says drinks is seven cents and Jamie said I just seen you sell one to *him* for a nickel, speaking about a white man setting there."

"Then what happen?" Henry asked, a pain pushing inward at his chest.

"The man say drinks cost a nickel for gas customers, seven cents for niggers who don't own a car."

"Then that devil Jamie haul off and spit on him!" Miss Maul shrieked.

Henry closed his eyes and saw it, saw Jamie spit on the white man, saw the shocked faces of the men at the filling station become angry as they stood up and moved toward Jamie; saw Jamie's anger turn to fear as he backed away; heard him apologize when it was too late for apologies; saw the boy eyes wishing they were back home plowing the field in the hot sun.

"Then they whip him!" Miss Maul said gleefully.

"They take him by the arms and walk him out to the man's garage behind the filling station," Trace said. "Not one colored man was left on the street to find out what happen by the time they reach the garage. Then they take him in the back and lay him down on the floor and bring a big strop . . ."

"Leather. Like goes under the bellies of plow mules," Miss Maul said.

"Then they beat him till they bring blood, and all the time he praying and crying and begging," Trace added.

Henry held back a sob and slowly set his glass on the table. "What happen next?" he asked, his voice hoarse.

"They tell him the highway points north and put him in the back of a pickup and rode him up to highway 82 and put him out. They told him to keep going, he wants to live."

Henry stood up and hesitated for only a moment, then he walked to the door. He fumbled in the dark for a latch, then opened the door and walked down the steps, listening for it to slam behind him. It slammed when he was halfway to the road. Miss Maul giggled loudly again, and he shuddered. He walked across the yard, his feet dragging. Behind him he heard Miss Maul's piercing giggles and Trace's hoarse voice. "Come on back here, Henry, and finish your whiskey. It makes you feel better."

He shuddered again and kept walking, but Miss Maul's giggles were with him for several hundred yards. Although it had turned cool, his forehead sweated and wet the dust on his face. Just before he reached the place where the path angled off the road, a fox darted in front of him. It stopped in the center of the road, glanced at him for a minute, and leaped into the brush.

"That a bad sign for a fox to stop and look at a man," he said. He took out his handkerchief, trying to control his shaking hands. Then he wiped the dust and sweat from his face, blew his nose, and with his shirtsleeve, wiped the tears from his eyes.

It didn't take him long to reach the house. He was blowing hard and surprised at how fast he'd been walking, when he reached the barn. He walked around the dark house to the front porch. He stepped on one of Lavina's snuff bottles and felt it explode beneath his foot. Slowly he bent down and picked up the pieces and tossed them under the porch. The creak of Lavina's rocker was the only sound.

"Your supper is cold, waiting for you on the table," she said.

"I ain't hungry," he replied. "Where the girls?" he asked.

"I let them go over to the schoolhouse for awhile. You find out where Jamie is?"

He walked to the steps and sat down. Slowly he removed his shoes and stretched his aching feet. He could smell the strong odor of the cape jasmine from the bush in the yard. "Jamie gone north," he said. "Maybe he'll find my brother and aunt in Chicago."

Lavina stopped rocking for only a minute, then continued, back and forth.

20

Seldom Sung Songs

Ouida was still in the parlor, now crocheting the cuffs on a dress she was making for Hazel's baby, when Tom pulled up in the drive.

At last she felt calm, at peace. As if, in a way, Perce really had come home at last and brought out the light thoughts and feelings that had lain buried in the recesses of her mind for years like furniture hidden by dust covers in a closed and locked room.

She waited for Tom to come into the room where the coffin rested, surprised that she no longer resented the intrusion as she had earlier in the day. She knew that she had been right when she'd told Camilla that, in his way, Tom had loved Perce; had loved all of them, even if his was a demanding, selfish, taking love. He knew no other kind.

He nodded at her, crossed the room, and sat down in the overstuffed, wine colored velvet chair, where Aunt Iola had spent the afternoon. He knew—how could he not know?—that Kiki was home.

"Where is she?" he asked after awhile, his gaze fixed on the coffin.

"I let her go to that doings at the high school tonight. After thinking it over, I didn't see the harm in it. And I let that soldier escort her. I wanted him out from under foot, and besides, Camilla didn't want to be escorted by Progress Whittal." Ouida wasn't deliberately being evasive; her mind was at the ball with Camilla. She wondered if she really might win. Her heart had seemed set on it. In fact, she'd sent Lavina down to the store to stuff twenty dollars, when no one was looking, in the container they had for her down there by the cash register. Maybe, she thought, she should have given Lavina more. After all, if the thing was to be bought, there was no reason she couldn't have bought it for her own daughter. Certainly she had neglected her wants and wishes far too long.

"I wasn't talking about Camilla," Tom said.

"Yes, I just had my mind on Camilla. She went with them. Drove them over there in her car."

"What's she like?" Tom asked.

Remembering the conversation with Kiki at the church, it was hard for Ouida to answer.

"She's a lot like your father was," Ouida answered.

"She always did favor him," he said and dismissed the subject. Ouida wondered why he didn't ask her how long she'd known that Kiki was coming home. Perhaps he already knew.

"He didn't like me very much, did he?" Tom said, still looking at the coffin.

"No," Ouida answered. "Camilla said the same thing this morning, not in so many words, and I defended you."

"Why?" he asked.

"Because it was what I wanted to believe."

Tom was silent for a long time, and Ouida returned to her crocheting. Then he turned and looked at her closely before speaking.

"I wonder why I'm not mad at her? I'd of thought I'd wanted to kill her if I could ever have imagined such a thing could be done to me."

Ouida bit off the thread. "Probably for the same reason that I'm not mad at you."

"I'm not looking forward to facing her."

"You will, though. Just as I've had to face you all these years when you've come home after being off two and three days at the time."

He quickly looked away.

"No, Tom. I don't hate you for that. I can't even think less of myself for putting up with it. I became accustomed to putting up with it. I think you can accustom yourself to just about anything in life, if you feel you have to."

He carefully considered his next words. "I can't say that it will ever be any different."

"I know that. There was a time, when the children were little, that I put up with an awful lot from you. In your drinking days, when you were torn between—Well, I knew that you were torn between your duty here and your feelings for Mavis—" She stopped for a moment, realizing it was the first time she had ever spoken her name in Tom's presence. "It was hard in those times."

"It's a wonder to me that you stayed with me. Now."

"Where did I have to go, Tom? A woman does not have the choices in life that a man has, not a woman with three children. I never felt I was strong enough to make such choices, at any rate."

"And you do now."

"Yes, Tom, I do now. I don't know why I do, and I'm not even sure that I understand why. But I do."

Again there was silence, as Tom stared at Perce's flag-draped coffin. "I wish I had taken the time to get to know him better."

"Yes," she said, standing up. Cars were pulling up in the drive. She left the room, closing the door behind her.

Bud and Hazel were in the first car. They got out and walked up the steps to where Ouida was waiting. "What happened?" she asked. "Did she win?"

"She won it," Hazel said.

"Oh, I'm so proud," Ouida replied.

"You wouldn't of been, if you'd been there," Bud said angrily.

"I'll bet she was so happy," Ouida said, ignoring him, as the second car pulled up to a stop.

"Mama, you ought not to have done it," Bud said.

"Done what?"

"Mama, how could you let her go off with that soldier, when you knew Progress was supposed to escort her?"

"I thought it was best," Ouida replied, wondering why the others were still sitting in Kiki's car.

"Well, you ought to make her learn to keep her promises," Bud said.

"I never been so embarrassed for anybody in my life. Poor Progress was wandering around that old gym like he just didn't know what to do, and Camilla didn't even give him as much as the time of day," Hazel said.

"I'm sure that Progress will get over it," Ouida said, as Kiki got out of the car and walked toward the house.

"She had a date to go with Progress—" Bud began.

"Camilla went with the date of her choice," Kiki said, starting up the steps.

"I guess you were back of the whole thing, weren't you?" Bud spat.

"I suppose, if anyone was back of anything, I must be the guilty party. But I really don't see why you are so upset," she smiled. Ouida knew, without being able to see in the dim light, that her eyes weren't smiling.

"Well, what did you do it for? She had a date with Progress. How do you think he felt?" Bud asked.

"Bud, I really don't give a damn how Progress felt. I was much more concerned about how Camilla felt. I would have thought she would be your concern too. But then, I can certainly understand *your* deep sympathy for Progress."

"Well, some people have got a lot of nerve, is all I got to say, and after I offered to loan her my yellow dress too. And some people have a nerve sticking their noses in other people's business, as far as that goes." That was Hazel.

"Which isn't far," Kiki said, lighting a cigarette.

"What do you mean by that?" Hazel asked. "I don't see what business you got barging in here and telling everybody what to do. Bud, I want you to know how this woman has upset me since she's been here, bossing everybody around. Why she has upset me so much she is going to make my baby come prematurely, that is what she is going to do!"

"Oh, for the love of Christ," Kiki said. "For the past several hours, all I've heard out of you is your precious condition and your baby. The way you carry on, you'd think you were carrying Jesus Christ, himself. You're not the first woman to ever have a baby."

"You be quiet!" Bud hissed.

"I don't have to be quiet," Kiki answered.

"Please. Now stop this," Ouida said, glancing at the front door.

"Well, I may not be the first woman to ever have a baby; but at least mine will have a father," Hazel barged on.

Kiki smiled again. "And just what do you mean by that?"

"You know what I'm talking about."

"Why don't you just come right out and say it?"

Rapidly losing her nerve, but having gone too far to stop, Hazel continued: "Well, at least my baby won't be a bastard like yours was, and it won't be born in some ditch!"

"At last," Kiki said, taking the cigarette between her thumb and forefinger and advancing toward Hazel's face with it. "I've looked forward to this since the first moment I laid eyes on you . . ."

Hazel screamed and ran behind Bud for protection. Bud grabbed Kiki's arm.

"Take your hands off me, young man," she ordered.

Camilla, followed by a reluctant James Lyon Hansen, rushed up into the yard.

"What's happening?" Camilla asked.

"Just a little family misunderstanding," Kiki answered. "This porch has seen plenty of them. Anyway, I thought you two were going on to the senior party. When you get an offer to borrow my car, you'd better take it."

Camilla looked at James Lyon, who was staring at Kiki, his mouth open.

"Don't just stand there, goof. You heard what she said. Anyway, you look like you're catching flies, with your mouth open like that."

"Well, go on," Kiki said.

"Come on, goofball," Camilla said, taking his arm. "Let's go. You don't mind, do you, Mama?"

"Go ahead," Ouida said, quietly.

They watched Camilla and James Lyon walk back to the car, then Bud turned on Kiki, his face flushed: "Just who in the hell do you think you are, lady? Coming around here and ordering everybody around and trying to attack my wife? I know what you are! Everybody knows what you are! *Everybody* knows what you are!" he repeated.

"What am I Bud?" she asked, sounding almost bored.

He stared at her, beginning to lose his nerve completely: "It beats all . . . It just beats all I ever heard of, that's what it does. Hell, if you don't know what you are—"

"I'll ask you again, Bud. What am I?"

"You got some damn nerve! Coming in a man's house when his son is laid out—"

"Shut up, Bud. You're going to bring your father out here," Ouida said.

"I want to bring him out here!"

Tom opened the screen door and stepped onto the porch. "I am out here," he said. "I been standing here the whole time enjoying the show."

"Daddy, throw this woman out on her ass. She tried to burn my wife with a lit cigarette."

"She *did* Daddy Kantwith!" Hazel shrieked.

"Oh, hell, Hazel. If she'd really wanted to harm you, she would have. Bud, take your wife and go to bed."

"She—" Bud began.

"You heard what I said, didn't you, boy?"

Bud looked from Tom to Kiki and back to Tom. "This beats all. It just beats all I ever heard of."

"Take Hazel and go to bed," Tom ordered. "You never were even in the battle, but you still ain't got sense enough to know when you've been beat."

"Have you, Tom?" Ouida asked.

"I have," he replied. "Now all of you go on. I want to talk to my sister, and tomorrow's a long day coming."

"Ouida, would you turn off the porch lights?" Tom asked. Only Kiki saw her smile.

"You tricked me, Prissy," Tom said.

"Yes," Kiki replied. "You want to sit down?"

"Steps fine with you?"

"Yes."

"You really did," Tom said, as the two of them sat down on the top step. "You come in for the kill. When Old Man . . . When Donald Goodwin told me it was you—I could have killed you when I found out it was you."

"I figured that thought would cross your mind. What made you change it?"

"Everything that has happened. The boy in there. Bringing my son home. Prissy, he was my oldest son. And he died hating me. I know that. And you're my sister. You hate me, and you got every reason to. You've ruined me, but I'm still man enough . . .

"Man enough to know when I've been bested. And I still got pride enough to admit I'm glad it was by one of my own. By my own sister.

"Pride. What an evil thing is a man's pride. It's made fools of better men than me, Prissy. When I found out today that I was not the richest man in this part of the world but the poorest, I came to see how little difference it made. It's a terrible thing for a man to find that out when he's my age."

Tom took out a cigarette, but didn't light it. "A dynasty. That's what we try to build. It's the way of us here in this part of the world, always has been. Every mother's son of us want to found a dynasty in one generation. Over and over we try it, and over and over we fail, trying to leave something behind us so that we will be remembered by a bunch of damn fools that couldn't care less once you're gone.

"Time and again we send our sons off to seek glory for our own pride. Time and again they come back in a box, if they come back at all." He took out a match and lit the cigarette.

"It's the way of the South, to send her sons off to glory. Our damnable pride makes us do it. Look how many times we've done it. We send the best off or drive them away from us, and they never come back. If we end up with our dynasty, most never have any sons left to leave it to.

"My son there in his box. He was the best, but I never took time to know it. And when a man loses a son like that . . . and especially if that son hates you!

"My god. He's lost a part of his *self*. A son like that is what carries on a man's name after he is gone. It's what makes a man immortal. We've fooled ourselves into thinking it's the land that lasts, but it's not. It's the blood. The blood a man passes on is what makes him immortal.

"Immortal! That preacher over yonder at Hebron can rave and rant til doomsday about his immortality, but he don't know the first damned thing about it.

"Immortality.

"My son Perce.

"He was not a hero, Katherine. He was a soldier, killed in a war with none to remember him but us here, and he fathered no sons to carry on his name, his blood. And that Chinaman who shot and killed my son? Who is to remember his name or know it? But he killed a part of me. Maybe the best part. He was the flesh of my flesh, and while he lay there where he was killed the last two years, I ran around making a fool of myself, trying to build a dynasty for *him*. And him already dead."

"You have another son. You have Camilla. Bud will give you a grandson," Kiki said.

"Breeding is a very precarious thing, Prissy. I'm not putting much stock on anything that comes from Bud's loins and Hazel's womb. Bud is too much like me. He will spend the best part of his life chasing greed.

"What I'm saying, Prissy, is that I know what I did to you, that night here. What I took from you. I hurt for it, Prissy. I've hurt a long time for it. *Damn* pride. I've never forgiven myself. But what I'm asking is, can you ever forgive me?"

Kiki turned and looked at him. She could see tears glistening on his cheeks in the moonlight. "I don't know, Tom. I really don't know."

Seated at the organ, Ouida finally remembered the old song that Lavina had taught her, and she began playing it. She didn't care if the whole household thought she had gone mad; she played it with all the volume she could force out of the contrary old machine.

Lavina, still sitting on her front porch, heard the music and stood up. She walked down the steps and across the yard, washed by the light of a May moon. Then she began singing with the music, her strong voice firm and free:

Shine on mighty river
Carry my sorrows to sea
Shine on mighty river
Angels cry for me.

It's a hard land we've come to
Full of burden, full of wrongs
Whisper dark river, sing to me
Softly now sing, your seldom sung songs.

Shine on mighty river
Let the moon wash away my tears
Shine on mighty river
The Angels will take my fears.

I'll face a new day tomorrow
No more heartache, no more tears

Shine on mighty river
Softly now sing, your seldom sung songs.

For me, for me
Shine on mighty river
Sing your seldom sung songs
for me . . . for me . . .